SECRETS OF LIFE EVERY TEEN NEEDS TO KNOW

**By Terry L. Paulson, Ph.D.
and Sean D. Paulson**

Copyright © 1990 Terry L. Paulson
Joy Publishing
San Juan Capistrano, California

Library of Congress Cataloging-in-Publication Data

Paulson, Terry L. 1945-
Secrets of life every teen needs to know / by Terry L.
Paulson and Sean D. Paulson.
   p. cm.
ISBN 0-939513-42-0
1. Teenagers -- Conduct of life. 2. Youth -- United States
-- Attitudes. 3. Adolescent. I. Paulson, Sean D. 1971- II.
Title.
CIP 90-63405

SECRETS OF LIFE EVERY TEEN NEEDS TO KNOW
Published by: Joy Publishing
P.O. Box 827, San Juan Capistrano, California 92675

Printed in the United States of America

First edition published in 1990
Current edition's most recent printing is indicated by the
first digit below:
1 2 3 4 5 6 7 8 9 10

WHO DESERVES THANKS?

Thank you:

Sharon Riding for your editing, assistance and support,

Woody Young for your generous support and publishing expertise,

Kathy Smith and Dynatype for your cover design,

Gooseart Publications for your fun graphics,

Dan Poynter for your professional assistance,

All the teens and parents who provided their input and ideas, especially those from the Agoura High School class of 1990,

Ann and Homer Paulson for your skill and persistence in first lecturing and loving the older author,

Nicole Bauer for your loving support to the younger author,

Librarians and booksellers everywhere for the spaces in your places,

Finally, our Father in heaven for his inner support and guidance that we hope is reflected in these pages.

But this book is dedicated to the only person it could be dedicated to--Lorie. Thank you for being so special to us both.

"If you find mistakes in this publication, please consider that they are there for a very good reason. We publish something for everyone...and some people are always looking for mistakes." Jim Gentil

What's in This Book?

LIVING ON THE SAFE SIDE

LIVING OUT THE BIG PICTURE

FINISH HERE!

AUTHORS' FIRST WORDS

Good Morning, Good Afternoon, and Good Night:

As the cool half of this writing duo (The teen half of course), let me tell you what you're probably thinking before you say it: "A teen helped write this! You've got to be joking! He must have sold out to agree to any of these lectures!" Well, there is no truth to that. First, these are 23 lessons of life teens we surveyed selected as the ones they "would most want to live by." They are not just my parents' sermons. Second, my dad and I worked evenings and even went away on a weekend retreat to write this book together. Each of us would take time to write our own advice, we'd compare notes, discuss them, and then use my dad's version! Yeah right! Don't worry; that's not the whole story.

Both of us tried to write the chapters from the parents' point of view; mine being from the sane and just parent. After all, that's what the book is--a book of timeless secrets most parents don't take the time to share but should. At least what you read has been changed to get the "Sean Seal of Approval." I did my best to make sure that we kept the advice realistic. I must admit, the more I worked on the chapters, the more sense they made to me.

I sometimes feel a little guilty, because I don't even use all the advice on these pages myself. Which is another way of saying, "I've heard good old number.... more times than I want to remember." But they still have a way of staying in my mind. When I worked with kids for the YMCA, I heard myself repeating some of the same lectures my parents had given me. I still have a long way to go to be the adult I want to be. I'll be growing along with you.

As Billy Joel said, "We didn't start the fire." This book is here to keep you from getting burned in this sometimes crazy world we didn't get to create. All the answers are not in this book, but many of the ones that will help get you through are here. The others are out there for you to find yourself. I enjoyed representing the teen generation on this writing team. I hope you enjoy reading and using it.

Sean D. Paulson

Dear Reader:

Like most fathers, I have always felt compelled to pass on to my son the "wisdom" I have collected over the years. I want to help him avoid the pitfalls I have experienced along the way. Just because he has trouble hearing my wisdom does not diminish my need or responsibility to share it anymore than it did for my dad or for fathers or, for that matter, mothers through the ages.

No one has ever said growing up is easy for any generation, and it isn't getting any easier. The combination of the seemingly self-destructive behavior of so many teens and the crazy world they are having to grow up in has placed the outcome of the journey into question. No wonder so many parents and teens feel hopeless and helpless. We trust that your beginning to read this book will prove to be one of many constructive steps in taking charge of your own future.

Any book that takes on the goal of communicating the "secrets of life" can't ever really be finished, so we're publishing it as it is. There are too many pleading for us to get it out! We've talked about it for three years, struggled to write it, collected quotes, surveyed and talked to teens and parents alike, and fine-tuned the messages until we're tired of editing them. It's time for you to be the judge as to the effectiveness of our efforts.

Use this book for what it's designed--as a resource guide to help you explore some of the timeless life lessons we've all had to struggle to learn. It's not a definitive answer to all of life's problems, but it will stimulate your mind and open you and your family to lessons all of us can learn from. Even if you don't agree with all we've written, it will lead you to think about values few in America seem to find time to even look at.

Let us know what you find. We surveyed hundreds of teens and parents to do this book. By filling out "The Test" in the back of this book, you and your family can be part of the next revision. It allows you to register your family's favorite lectures, the ones your parents most often give, and the ones you, as a teen, most want to grow up to live by. It also provides space for you to write some of your own favorite lectures we may not have included. We thank you in advance for taking the time to read and use our book. May you enjoy and benefit from reading it.

Terry L. Paulson

Attention schools, churches, public an private organizations:
This book is available at quantity discounts with bulk purchase for educational, promotional, or fund-raising purposes. For further information, refer to the "Now, What Can We Do for You?" section at the back, or contact Paulson & Associates Inc., at P.O. Box 365, Agoura Hills, CA 91301 (818)991-5110

START HERE!

If you do not start here, you will not pass "Go" and you will not collect $200. If you do start here and somehow receive $200, send us a small share!

"Why read this parental propaganda? I mean, do I really have to read this stuff?" We can hear the complaints ringing through the high school hallways across America. "I've already heard these lectures from my parents, and now I have to read it too! Next you'll have me memorizing the numbers!" All right, we don't expect this book to jump onto the teen best seller list without at least a fight. **But if you've chosen to read this far, maybe there are some things you can salvage from reading further. After all, there are some tried and true secrets of life adults through the ages have learned in making life work.** OK, not even all the adults have learned some of these. The fact remains, in a very few years you will be an adult. It may be worth your time to struggle with some of the time-tested secrets of life that few adults take the time to even share. Most adults will admit there are many things they wish they had learned as a teen. You will get to do just that!

It isn't just parents that think these lessons are important. **When surveyed on favorite family lectures, hundreds of teens picked the 23 lessons included in this book as the lessons of life they most wanted to live by.** Give this book a chance; even your peers think it's worth reading.

This book is not designed to make teenagers "perfect." The only place that perfect people exist are in the movies. That's because they can edit out all the errors and put make-up over all the flaws. All parents made their own mistakes as teens, just as all generations through the ages have done. They've even made more than their share of mistakes as adults. We in the Paulson clan, like you, have gone or are going through the eighteen-year experiment as parents and child with no dress rehearsals and more than our quota of mistakes.

There have been many family lectures through the years--some listened to and some not. Some have passed by the wayside unable to stand the test of our changing times. All we have included in this book have been repeated often enough to become family standards in many homes across America. The lectures included in this book are not just our lectures. We went beyond our family to include lectures from other families. We then gave questionnaires to hundreds of teenagers and parents to establish the top 46 lectures in their homes. Our censors have had to edit out some of the more creative versions submitted. **For the teen book we limited the list to the 23 lectures teens felt were the most important to live by. These are the best of the**

best. Suffice it to say, this is not just our book. It's a collection of truths every family ought to be exposed to.

This book will help you struggle with ethics--the values and beliefs that you need to help direct your actions in an often troubled and always changing world. Every parent learns quickly that they can't control a child. In fact, they sometimes wonder whether the child is actually controlling them. But that still doesn't diminish a parent's responsibility to influence their teens positively. They still have a job to do to help develop your self-esteem, your skills, and your character. Hopefully, what is written on these pages will help them do just that.

> *"It's scary to think that I'll be out on my own in the real world very soon. I am just a kid trying to survive in high school, get good grades, have fun and still be a gentleman. I've got problems just like the next person, and I don't expect all of my questions to be answered. But lately I've started looking at myself more, and caring more about the man I am becoming. I realize that I've made mistakes, hurt people, lied and acted in a horrid manner to the people I love. I can only say, 'I'm sorry, but I'm still growing up'"*
> *Richard Laurence, high school student*

We hope this book goes beyond informing and stimulating. We hope it helps you and your parents to laugh at the things that happen in your home. Most parents and teens make it through to adulthood with only minor scars, and we often take ourselves and our struggles too seriously. After hearing some of the lectures other parents give, you may just echo the words of the younger author of this book, "After hearing some of the lectures other parents give, I realize you're not so bad!"

> *"Truth is a river that is always splitting up into arms that reunite. Islanded between the arms the inhabitants argue for a lifetime as to which is the main river." Cyril Connolly*

Writing our short "generic" lectures proved more difficult than we had expected. It was an exercise in family discovery. We had to ask ourselves some difficult questions: What do we really believe? How do we include the views of other parents and teens? How do you say it in a constructive way that would make sense to teens? How can you mesh the views of a parent and a vocal teen into one message both could agree on? How do you get an aging father to write in a "hip" way? It was not easy.

16

As you will notice in reading the lectures, we tried to limit the slang that might date the message and make it impossible for parents to understand. The conversation, *"Yar! Dude! Check out that P.P.D."* "Reverse gears! Dude! She's nuked." *"You Hemorrhoid!"* may make sense to many teens. But parents need a quick translation into slang they can understand: *"Cool! Man! Check out that chick (Potential Prom Date)!"* "Makes me want to puke; looks like her hair is blow dried in a microwave!" *"Don't be a pain!"* Maybe we can end this digression with a slang lecture to go with our family favorites, *"Pull a clue out of the clue bag!"* or for your parents, "Think sensibly. Don't be stupid."

Limiting the slang was not our only compromise. At Sean's suggestion, we tried to limit our lectures to messages that could be read in less than ten minutes. We figured the longest the average teen can listen to anything from a parent is ten minutes, and that might be pushing it. No matter what the length of the lecture, if you find yourself disagreeing with some of the thoughts expressed, you can blame our family, and us alone. We don't apologize for any of the lectures. We hope that even if you disagree, it provides a launching pad for a healthy discussion in your family or with your friends. **Now, if you really can't stand this book, all is not lost. You can give it anonymously to someone you can't stand!**

"All generalizations are dangerous, even this one." Alexander Dumas

Now, how can you use this book? Try reading and reacting to the lectures individually or as a family. **This book is not meant to be read in one sitting; there's no rush! Reading too many lectures in a row might make anyone want to**

throw up. The book is best used in small doses in response to issues you or your family are facing. Some lessons you may never need to read; you may have been living the lesson without need of your parents' advice or the advice of this book. Some messages, on the other hand, may hit a responsive chord. You may need to read and re-read that chapter until the pages are frayed at the edges. Don't worry; it is designed to be your book to be used as needed.

While this resource book is not designed as a workbook, feel free to make it one. Make the lectures yours by adding your own words and quotes in the margins. You may even need to skip some of the lectures you most disagree with, but don't rip them out. Three years from now you may decide those same lessons are closer to the truth than you wanted to admit. It is true there is no one blueprint for success, but give each of the lessons a chance to grow on you.

> *"A quotation at the right moment is like bread to the famished."*
> The Talmud

> *"Ethical axioms are found and tested not very differently from the axioms of science. Truth is what stands the test of experience."*
> Albert Einstein

> *"In the purest form, truth is not a polite tap on the shoulder. It is a howling reproach. What Moses brought down from Mount Sinai were not the Ten Suggestions."* Ted Koppel

If you don't like one of the chapters as written, take a page and write your own version and give it to your parents as a way to open discussion on an alternative point of view. You might even try using one of the lessons to stimulate an entry in your diary.

Your parents can and will learn from you. Give them a chance to hear and understand your own thoughts and feelings. You may be surprised at how well they listen when you give them a chance. **By making regular, open conversations a habit, problems won't be as likely to build up into open warfare in the home.**

Don't forget that parents are only people. They haven't got all the answers. Keep these four thoughts in mind. **First, believe that they care and will always care for you even if their actions don't always make you feel that way. Second, instead of thinking about how much they haven't done for you, think of all they have done. Third, find your own way to say you love your parents; they need to know that. Finally, no matter what happens within your family, you are a one-of-a-kind creation of a loving God who will never desert you.**

"The right way to begin is to pay attention to the young, and make them just as good as possible." Socrates

"We cannot always build the future for our youth, but we can build our youth for the future." Franklin D. Roosevelt

"America grew great from the seed of the will to do and dare; the will to get up and go on and not to quit after we had erred and fallen; and will to struggle to our feet and plod along and not to give up and lie down when we wavered and stumbled from fatigue. It grew not from the seed of slumping down and giving in when laden with apparent discouragement and seeming defeat, but from

the seed of the will to rise to the occasion, shake it off, stand firm and resolute, and challenge defeat. Yes, it seems what we in America need is to get back to the planting and cultivating of that good old American seed." Arnold W. Craft

"When I was a boy of fourteen, my father was so ignorant I could hardly stand to have the old man around. But when I got to be twenty-one, I was astonished by how much the old man had learned in seven years." Mark Twain

You are the future, but there is no reason you can't begin to make a difference today! Welcome to our feast--23 time-tested secrets of life every teen needs to know. We hope you enjoy reading and digesting them as much as we enjoyed writing them. Now, **until further notice, celebrate life!**

1

Take Pride in Who You Are--You Are Unique

"The only man who never makes a mistake is the man who never does anything." Theodore Roosevelt

Lincoln's entry in a childhood copy book: "Abraham Lincoln, his hand and pen. He will be good but god knows When."

"At dinnertime, dad (Harpo Marx) would begin his nightly ritual by raising his forefinger and intoning, 'And in conclusion...' Then we would go around the table reviewing our triumphs and trials of the day. Dad fielded gripes by reducing tragedy to absurdity. Soon you were laughing at yourself, and your problems faded away. He was a born healer." Bill Marx, son of Harpo Marx

Maintaining your own self-esteem is an inside job. Only you can make your potential blossom. Only you can waste the unique gifts you have been given.

"No one can make me feel inferior but myself." Eleanor Roosevelt

"Calm self-confidence is as far from conceit as the desire to earn a decent living is remote from greed." Channing Pollock

Instead of giving in to the teenage "ego yo-yo" learn to believe in yourself! Without a humble but realistic self-confidence, it is hard to be successful or happy. But how do you build a realistic self-confidence? It's important to look at what you do to lose your confidence to understand how to improve it.

"If I am not for myself, who will be for me? If I am only for myself, what am I? And if not now, when?" Rabbi Hillel

Look at your self-confidence as the collection of all the things you say to yourself about yourself. Unfortunately, most of us are far from kind in what we say inside our minds. A mistake is often worth 45 minutes of self-whipping spread over a three-day period. How many times have you said to yourself: "That was stupid! Why did I say that? And they were all watching me--I'm sure they are going home thinking about my mistake!" "If God found out what I did, I'm history. I mean zap--a sidewalk pizza right there!" Then your personal filer goes back to all your past failures! It's as if your mind says, "You're right boss; you are stupid. Remember the time you..." Like most of us, you lose sleep over the really bad mistakes.

Now what do you say to yourself when you do something right? "It was a fluke!" "They could do it better." "It's about time!" Even when you do feel good, it doesn't last long. You don't lose sleep over the good ones! **Most of us are far more critical than we are supportive in our internal conversations.**

"People are so used to seeing what's missing, they fail to see what's there." Anonymous

To add to the problem, we look at a world that presents itself as perfect--look good, cover your mistakes, hide those blemishes. It's so easy to see other teens as being **so** pretty, **so** sharp, so confident! **We compare our own tarnished image of ourselves to the polished public images**

of others. We lose that comparison! We lose badly! Enough of the problem; you can do something.

"If we were able to accomplish what we're capable of doing we'd astonish ourselves." Thomas Edison

"Never let a careless remark someone made years ago affect who you are today." Anonymous

You don't have to be anyone but yourself. **There is no standardized model; there has never been anyone like you. You are unique and special.** You don't have to be the

best-dressed, best-mannered, best-cultured, best-adjusted or best-anything teenager on the block. You don't have to be on any honor roll for people to love you. Being a brilliant "A" student isn't everything; some of those who have done poorly in school have been great successes outside of school. You don't have to be a super athlete. You're better in **some way** from **every** person you meet. You have to find what you're good at and what you like doing and then develop those strengths. Your uniqueness brings with it a responsibility. **You have a job to do in this world, and if you don't do it, it will never be done.** The world can't afford to miss what you have to offer. You are called by a name; do that name proud.

> *"God made us all different for a good reason. An orchestra would be pretty dull if everyone played the same instrument. There are enough big mouths in the world. But not enough good listeners. You're so busy counting what you don't have, you're not counting what you do have." Anonymous*

> *"Do what you can, with what you have, where you are." Theodore Roosevelt*

Now that you know that you are unique, **learn to talk to yourself the way you talk to people you care about.** Don't take yourself for granted. Catch yourself being effective daily--what did you do today you handled well? Write it in your calendar or diary. **If you're not catching yourself being effective, you may be winning and not know it because you're not keeping score.**

> *"An occasional compliment is necessary, to keep up one's self-respect.... When you cannot get a compliment any other way pay yourself one." Mark Twain*

All this positive talk does not mean life will always be full of smiles. You will still have bad days; embarrassing things happen to everybody. But you can learn to make every error an opportunity to grow instead of an invitation for self-whipping. Life is like a moving vehicle with no brakes;

24

if you spend too much time in the rearview mirror, you will hit a tree out the front window. **Get out of your internal rearview mirror! Identify what you did wrong then focus on the future--What you are going to do to fix the problem? Then, how will you handle a similar situation next time?** Remember, it's always easier to admit you made a mistake than to admit you are one. Learn from your errors and then let go. You can't change the past; it's over. Remember that most of those embarrassing moments you worry about now will be some of your favorite stories you will love telling your children and grandchildren. Since you will laugh then, you might as well laugh now.

> *"If you fall, boy, you don't have to wallow. Ain't nobody going to think you somebody unless you think so yourself. Don't listen to their talk, boy, they don't have a pot to pee in or a window to throw it out. For God's sake, Jesse, promise me you'll be somebody. Ain't no such thing as 'cain't,' 'cain't' got drowned out in a soda bottle. Don't let the Joneses get you down. Nothing is impossible for those who love the Lord. Come hell or high water, if you got guts, boy, ain't nothing or nobody can turn you around." Matilda Burns, "Aunt Tibby", Jesse Jackson's grandmother*

> *"There are no failures, just results. Now get busy doing what you can to make your results better." Pat Riley*

Remember, behind it all, **God doesn't create junk.** Have faith in God that you will find a realistic faith in yourself. If you have faith, take time regularly to read the affirmations of God and you will trade your sense of insecurity for thoughts of faith and courage. Everyone has a place in His plan. God knows the worst about you, and loves you anyway. **Don't be programmed by the negativity of the world. No one is perfect, but all have value.**

"Don't let anyone think little of you because you are young.... Be sure to use your abilities God has given you.... Put those abilities to work; throw yourself into your tasks so that everyone may notice your improvements and progress." 1 Timothy 4:12-14

"In confidence and quietness shall be your strength." Isaiah 30:15

Even if you do not add up as the best at athletics, at school, or in any specific area, **you can always major in character--be known for your honesty, kindness, friendliness, and godliness. No one can take your character away; that makes you extremely important.** Your parents will frequently be frustrated by your actions, but behind those momentary feelings you will find an enduring love. Holding onto that love, your job as a teenager is to find and refine yourself into the person you are capable of becoming. Welcome to that challenge of finding your special place.

"I want to remind you to stir into flame the strength and boldness that is in you, that entered into you when I laid my hands upon your head and blessed you. For the Holy Spirit, God's gift, does not want you to be afraid of people, but to be wise and strong, and to love them and enjoy being with them. If you stir up this inner power, you will never be afraid...." 2 Timothy 1:6-7

"One of the basic laws of human existence is: find yourself, know yourself, be yourself." Norman Vincent Peale

2

Do the Best You Can

"All things come to those who hustle while they wait." Thomas Edison

Taking pride in who you are and striving to be the best you can be, does not mean you have to make it to the Olympics to count in this world. Far from it; only a few can realistically hope to achieve such an honor. "Being the best you can be" has more to do with believing in yourself and searching to find and develop your own strengths and uniqueness. That is a personal journey that only you can take. There may be no medals to win, but you will discover great satisfaction in the attempt. The biggest disappointment would be if you failed to even take the journey. **Never settle for being less than you are capable of being. You cheat all those around you, but most of all you cheat yourself.**

"Whatever you have, you must either use or lose." Henry Ford

"Every calling is great when greatly pursued." Oliver Wendell Holmes, Jr.

The first lesson to learn is that you can't expect to be the "best" at everything. Pick your areas to achieve carefully. Learn to listen to your heart and your mind--what do you enjoy doing? What are you good at? Don't try to become a master at everything and fail to master anything. It takes

27

time to become a master, that's why investing your time wisely is so important.

> *"The quality of a person's life is in direct proportion to their commitment to excellence, regardless of their chosen field of endeavor." Vince Lombardi*

The second lesson is equally important, make sure you are working on your own dreams. Many will encourage you, but don't let their encouragement drive you to discouragement by forcing you into areas you don't even enjoy. Don't let anyone force goals on you. Find and communicate your own dreams, and then let others help you get there. Everyone must take their own journey in life, and that is the way it should be. Learn from every person you respect, young or old alike. Take from each the qualities you want to adopt and make yours. Then add your own touches to make it uniquely you.

> *"There is perhaps no greater drain on human energy, creativity, and spirit than people 'misfit' in the work they do. Finding the right livelihood is a gift to the planet--a part of doing your share." Marie Arapakis*

> *"Let everyone be sure that he is doing his very best, for then he will have the personal satisfaction of work well done, and won't need to compare himself with someone else. Each of us must bear some faults and burdens of his own. For none of us is perfect!" Galations 6:4-5*

Being your best will not be easy; you will have setbacks. **Learn to let go of temporary disappointments and bounce back with renewed effort.** Being your best is more than saying the words; it requires sustained effort over time to master any job. You'll find progress easier when you keep large expectations trimmed down to manageable steps.

Getting good grades in science is a worthwhile goal, but if you have been a particularly poor student, that's a little like starting playing basketball with the Lakers. You walk across America one step at a time.

motivation

Break your dreams of being the "best" into small steps. Take the first step today.

"The important thing in the Olympic Games is not to win but to take part, the important thing in life is not the triumph but the struggle, the essential thing is not to have conquered but to have fought well. To spread these precepts is to build up a stronger and more valiant and above all a more scrupulous and more generous humanity." De. Coubertin

"The aim, if reached or not, makes the life great: Try to be Shakespeare, leave the rest to fate." Robert Browning

Don't forget to keep God in this equation. God doesn't create junk. You have a unique place in His plan. In our age of glitter and style, it is too easy to stand in awe of the skills of others while failing to even see or appreciate the skills you have. Don't wait for anyone to point out your skills, start discovering them yourself. **God has given you gifts; don't hide or waste them.**

> *"Use the abilities God has given--put them to work." I Timothy 4:14-15*

> *"Whatever your hand finds to do, do it with all your might." Ecclesiastes 9:10*

Unfortunately, there is no instruction plan anyone can give you. You can't find your unique skills in isolation. You will find it when you actively pursue life and all its opportunities. **While exploring life, some things will naturally strike a resonant chord and you will know it--"That's me and I love it!" Then all you will have to do is find a way to make what you're best at useful.**

> *"True discipline isn't on your back needling you with imperatives; it is at your side, nudging you with incentives. When you understand that discipline is self-caring, not self-castigating, you won't cringe at it's mention, but will cultivate it." Sybil Stanton*

> *"Sustaining effort is the most important thing for any enterprise. The way to be successful is to learn how to do things right, then do them the same way every time. Players can't excel in every area, but they can strive to better themselves in the areas that we value most for each individual. Then we can show them what they need to do to have their Career Best Effort." Pat Riley, former coach of the LA Lakers*

I remember a cartoon where the top Indian "Rain Dancer" was asked what made him effective. His reply was worth highlighting: "I was born to boogie!" **Welcome to the challenge of finding out what you were born to do.**

> *"There are times when things seem so bad that you've got to grab your fate by the shoulders and shake it.... If you keep your nose to*

30

the grindstone and work at it, it's amazing how in a free society you can become as great as you want to be." Lee Iacocca

Whatever you decide, get very good at being you. No parent should expect more. When you take pride in yourself by doing your best, they'll be right along side of you beaming.

"Try not to be a man of success; but rather try to be a man of value."
Albert Einstein

"I dread success. To have succeeded is to have finished one's business on earth.... I like a state of continual becoming...with a goal in front and not behind." George Bernard Shaw

3

Take the Time to Give It a Try

"Healthy people go 'Yes,' 'No,' and 'Whooppee!' Unhealthy people go 'Yes, but,' 'No, but,' and 'No Whooppee!'" Eric Berne

"Things may come to those who wait, but only the things left by those who hustle." Abraham Lincoln

"I don't want to do it!" **"How are you going to know if you don't even try it?"** "I know I wouldn't like it! It's not me! Besides, I just can't." **"Where there's a will there's a way."** Have you heard that conversation before? Probably, and this most likely won't be the last. Teens certainly aren't alone in needing to listen to this lecture. **Some people fail to risk trying new things throughout their life.** They stand silently on the sidelines of life watching the world go by. Unfortunately, it does go by, along with all the wonderful opportunities they could have had but didn't experience. "Oh, how I wished I'd tried learning to play the piano!" "I could have been on the tennis team, if I'd only gone out for the team." Lost opportunities are something you don't have to major in.

"It takes half your life before you discover life is a do-it-yourself project." Napoleon Hill

One woman expressed her resistance uniquely, "I can't change! On the freeway of life, I'm in the slow lane looking for an offramp." Do you want that to be you? We certainly hope not. Driving was not originally you, but you were willing to **make it you** because it's a long way to walk! The same is true with so much of life. **Don't live your life in a rut settling for what you've always done instead of what you could do.** Give yourself the opportunity of trying as

much of life as you can. Building a history of trying new things keeps your life a never ending journey of discoveries.

not stand back shivering and thinking of the cold and danger, but jump in and scramble through as well as we can." Sidney Smith

One wise sage described a rut as "a coffin with the ends kicked out of it." Do yourself a favor by not letting ruts form early in your life. **Be a "rut breaker" by keeping your mind and your habits flexible and creative.** We're moving into a future where change is the name of the game. You can be a "changer," or you can wait until you are "changed."

"I never stopped trying. And I never tried stopping." Dolly Parton

"It's always too soon to quit." Steve Allen

"Our doubts are traitors, and make us lose the good we oft might win, by fearing to attempt." Shakespeare

Futurists suggest that the average high school graduate will have six careers in her lifetime. That's not jobs! That's careers! If you are interested in trying something new, take the time to do it. What's the worst that can happen? You might invest a small amount of time in an activity that ends up having little payoff. But most of us waste more time than that daily watching commercials on TV. **The potential cost of experimenting with what life has to offer is small compared to what can be gained.**

"Do not neglect the gift which is in you." I Timothy 4:14

"Life is like a 10 speed bicycle. Most of us have gears we never use." Charles Schultz

"I am not judged by the number of times I fail, but by the number of times I succeed, and the number of times I succeed is in direct

Never think of total commitment when approaching anything new, think of trying a few small steps. The need for
total commitment invites images of years of work which,
in turn, generates procrastination and stillborn dreams.
Don't make "trying something" such a momentous commitment. "Giving something a shot" is designed to sample
life to find "what turns your dreams on!" It's hard to know
what you want out of life in a vacuum. **You will learn best
and enjoy life more when you keep in touch with life's
options by sampling what it has to offer.**

*"If one's mind can conceive it and one's heart can believe it, one
can achieve it." Jesse Jackson*

*"You can't be afraid of failure. The greatest failure is not to try at
all. Do it." Debbi Fields of Mrs. Fields Cookies*

**You'll go farther in life if you can trade your "No! That's
just not me!" for "Sure! I'll give it a try!"** Don't let growing
up mean an end to your "rut breaking" habit. Put to rest
the adage, "You can't teach an old dog new tricks!". Hold
onto the expectation of life-long learning--"You become
an old dog when you stop doing new tricks!"

*"The galleries are full of critics. They play no ball. They fight no
fights. They make no mistakes, because they attempt nothing.
Down in the arena are the doers. They make mistakes because they
attempt many things. The person who makes no mistakes lacks
boldness and the spirit of adventure. He is the one who never, never
tries anything new. He is the brake on the wheel of progress. The
very fact that he tries nothing, takes no chances, does nothing
except criticize those who try is, perhaps, the biggest possible error
in a life-time." Anonymous*

4

Learn to have a Positive Attitude about Life

"I don't want you to mistake my calmness for patience. For two days I watched you sulk and mope around here acting very, very sad, and I let you do that. But now you're depressing me! If you want to be sad, go up to your room and be sad. Put on your sad music, put on your sad clothes, dance around the room sad. Have a 'sadfest.' But tomorrow is another day. You are going to wake up with a smile. You are going to have a 'smilefest.' Do you understand me?" The Bill Cosby Show

"Anybody who says 'life is easy' hasn't been here." Anonymous

"Failure is the fertilizer of success." Dr. Denis Waitley

Having a positive attitude requires a daily choice we all have to make. **Every morning when we get up we have a choice--be happy or unhappy.** Many choose to be happy and to celebrate God's gift of another day. Others seem to love to dwell on the obstacles instead of the opportunities.

"Worry is negative goal setting. It's thinking how you want things not to happen." Michael McKinley

"If you think you can, or if you think you can't, you are right." Henry Ford

Entertain this sobering thought--"Your happiness is not your parents' responsibility; it's yours!" Parents are not here to guarantee a happy, mirthful, problem free journey through your teen years. They are not to be your cheerleaders, social workers, or resident rah-rah experts. They are your parents, and they're here to help you master a way to navigate your own journey through the same ups and downs that everybody has had to find a way to face. Your own attitude will be a help or hindrance in making your journey successful.

> *"Success is not in getting on top; it's how you bounce on the bottom." Gen. George Patton*

> *"The traditional version tells us that there are two things you need to succeed: talent and hunger, or drive. I have added a third thing, and that is optimism. You can have all the talent in the world, but if you don't believe you can overcome failure, if you do not mentally rehearse success, then your talent and drive will come to nothing once you have been knocked down." Martin Seligman*

Even if they could, most parents would not sweep aside every hurdle you will encounter on your journey to adulthood. They might even throw in a few of their own to help you learn how to jump. Everyone grows through mild adversity. Your parents' job is to help you bounce back and avoid being crushed in the process. **You deserve the right to face your own problems and profit from overcoming them yourself.** Those who have learned to conquer their problems are more secure than those that have never faced them. Even though your parents won't eliminate your challenges, they can be your resident coach and cheerleader to encourage you and be a sounding board as you go through them. Don't be afraid to talk to them. Talking often provides perspective and makes it easier to bounce back. You will soon find you are not alone, even in your own home.

"I wept because I had no shoes, until I saw a man who had no feet." Ancient Persian Saying

"Athletics teaches you that you've got to overcome adversity. Nobody goes unbeaten every year, nobody makes every shot, no one sinks every putt. Everybody's going to have problems. I've been on top; I've been on the bottom. I've learned that success is never final; defeat is not fatal. Whether it's in business, on the field, or in your personal life, the person who copes with problems and uses them as motivation is going to be successful." Lou Holtz

The world seems to be full of "Pits People"--"School is the pits! My family's the pits! This city is the pits! You're the pits!" They choose to live life in a black hole. You can

always focus on the bad news, but somewhere people are making good news out of even the worst circumstances. **Everyone at times feels discouraged, but you just don't have to stay there long.** Get busy making your life better with whatever cards you're dealt. After all, that's all anyone can do. **Investing your "worry time" in action will pay off in some handsome rewards.** Real positive thinkers don't rest in hope or words of encouragement, they are realists who struggle, fight, and claw their way through to overcome whatever problems they encounter.

"Things turn out best for those who make the best of the way things turn out." John Wooden

"Today is a new day. You will get out of it just what you put into it.... If you have made mistakes, even serious mistakes, there is always another chance for you. And supposing you have tried and failed again and again, you may have a fresh start any moment you choose, for this thing that we call 'failure' is not the falling down, but the staying down." Mary Pickford

If you do face tough times, don't pick that time to make big decisions. It's not a time to give up. It is the time to get help. When things seem tough, sit tight and find someone you trust to help you figure it out. Sometimes it will be your parent, other times a minister or a trusted friend or even a teacher. Talk to someone; it will make a difference.

"Suicide is a permanent solution to a temporary problem." Abigail Van Buren

"That which you have lost doesn't matter: What is important is what you still have." Ludwig Huttman, doctor and founder of the Olympic Games for the Handicapped

Never leave God out of the equation. He is always there to listen and give you strength; be ready to call on him and his promises of strength and guidance. You have heard it said, "If God be for me, who can be against me?" "God being for you" doesn't mean there will always be good times. Sometimes bad things happen to good people, but God uses the tough times to help us become strong. **You can trust that no pit is so deep that God is not deeper still.** The world will at times bend you, but it won't break you if you learn to make the best of even your toughest times.

"Besides, what's the use of worrying? What good does it do? Will it add a single day to your life? Of course not! And if worry can't

even do such little things as that, what's the use of worrying over bigger things?" Luke 12:25-26

"It is said an Eastern monarch once charged his wise men to invent him a sentence to be ever in view, and which should be true and appropriate in all times and situations. They presented him the words, 'And this, too, shall pass away.' How much it expresses! How chastening in the hour of pride! How consoling in the depths of affliction!" Abraham Lincoln

"This is the day which the Lord has made; let us rejoice and be glad in it." Psalm 118:24

Not all depression is the result of a bad attitude. Severe depression in its most disabling forms may be biologically based. This isn't your normal dip in mood that seizes everyone at times; it's more intense and longer lasting. Does the slightest annoyance set off irrational tantrums followed by days of lying in bed, crying, too depressed to shower or get dressed? Do you lose your appetite for extended periods of time or do the opposite, eating more than usual and sleeping for long hours? Do you have a severely depressed parent or an early loss of either parent? Do you have recurrent thoughts of death or suicide?

If you find yourself answering in the affirmative to many of these questions, you may be left with more than the pain of depression. You will have the guilt of not being able to beat it. **A severely depressed teen cannot merely "cheer up" or "snap out of it." Yet severe depression can often be treated successfully with expert assistance including medication and counseling.** See your family doctor or local mental-health professional that has experience in working with depressed teens.

"People are now recognizing depression as an illness and not a character flaw." Dr. Robert Hirschfield, National Institute of Mental Health

Positive thinking isn't an invitation to resting; it's an invitation to action. Even when you're sad, you're usually on the verge of learning something. Stay focused on this central choice: Positive people get somewhere while negative people get nowhere. Never lose your sense of humor; humor provides the sun to burn away the clouds of worry. Even your worst days will make great stories you can tell your grandchildren. You can even make it worse with time--"I mean when I was your age, I remember the time I had to...."

Never settle for waiting for a good day to come your way. Make it a good day starting now.

"Most folks are about as happy as they make up their minds to be." Abraham Lincoln

"Get out of that slow lane. Shift into the fast lane. If you think you can't, you won't. If you think you can, there's a good chance you will. Even making the effort will make you feel like a new person. Reputations are made by searching for things that can't be done and doing them. Aim low: boring. Aim high: soaring." Richard Kerr

"Be pleasant until ten o'clock in the morning and the rest of the day will take care of itself." Elbert Hubbard

"God grant me the serenity to accept the things I cannot change, the courage to change the things I can and the wisdom to know the difference." Reinhold Niebuhr

5

Don't Take Yourself Too Seriously--Learn to Laugh a Little!

"A child with a good sense of humor has nothing to fear from this world." Anne Dillard

"Warning: Laughter may be hazardous to your illness." Nurses for Laughter

After God created Adam and Eve, He gave them a baby. Then to keep the whole thing from falling apart, he invented humor. Never consider growing up as an obligation to become serious. **Keep your sense of humor as a ready sidekick throughout your life.**

"The cheerful heart has a continual feast." Proverbs 15:15

"Humor is the great thing, the saving thing, after all. The minute it crops up, all our hardnesses yield, all our irritations and resentments flit away, and a sunny spirit takes their place." Mark Twain

"Why humor? Why not humor? I'd rather it be my ally than my enemy." Robert Orben

Too many adults have long forgotten the value of humor. They walk around looking like they are in pain all day. You know the ones; instead of their cars, they leave their faces *in park.* It isn't just adults that are guilty. Too many teenagers also mistakenly assume that it is "in" to be "serious." For them, being "cool" ends up looking "terminal cool." Don't let that be you. Leave room for laughter every day. **Take your school and your work seriously, but take yourself and problems lightly.** Remember, laughter is contagious and so is negativism. Which would you prefer to give to others? You know the answer--people love to be around people who make them laugh.

> *"Laughter is the shortest distance between two people." Victor Borge*

> *"He deserves Paradise who makes his companions laugh." Mohammed, The Koran*

> *"The best way to cheer yourself is to try to cheer somebody else up." Mark Twain*

Not all humor works. Some humor creates laughter at the expense of others. **Leave sarcasm and jokes that make fun of others out of your personal comedy repertoire.** You don't need them to be funny, and you may hurt someone badly.

> *"When someone blushes with embarrassment..., when someone carries away an ache..., when something sacred is made to appear common..., when someone's weakness provides the laughter..., when profanity is required to make it funny..., when a child is brought to tears..., or when everyone can't join in the laughter..., it's a poor joke!" Cliff Thomas*

The safest target for your humor will always be yourself. Learn to laugh at your errors and the world will laugh with you--not at you! Only the self-confident can admit their mistakes; laughing at your own errors will help you let go of mistakes and bounce back. It will also make you more popular. We all like to be with people who are comfortable with who they are--warts, pimples, and all.

"A laugh at your own expense costs you nothing." Mary H. Waldrip

"One of the great secrets of contentment is the refusal to take ourselves seriously. To laugh at ourselves, to stand aside, and in imagination, watch ourselves go by." Gilbert Hay

Laughter is also one of the natural tranquilizers of life. When things are going crazy, take a trip on the funny side of life. **Laughter provides an inner upper, an emotional massage, a new perspective for irritations and disappointments.** Learn to say to yourself and others, "Are we having fun yet?" "Is this candid camera?" "Don't worry;

be happy!" "The crisis of today is the boring history of tomorrow." "Some day this will be a great story!" Why cry when you can laugh? Before you think that such humor is only necessary for teenagers, let us put that thought to rest. All parents learn to say the same kind of messages to help them survive the eighteen year parenting experiment. My mother's favorite saying was, "This too shall pass." She was talking about me. We all need humor.

"What really works in life is being able to bounce back. Resilience--that's what does it. If you stop and think, nothing is as bad as it seems. In the worst moments, I've always found that something funny was happening. And for that I give my mother credit. Judy Garland could cry, but she was also one of the world's great laughers." Liza Minelli

"Be of good cheer; it is I. Don't be afraid." Matthew 14:27

"An inexhaustible good nature is one of the most precious gifts of heaven, spreading itself like oil over the troubled sea of thought, and keeping the mind smooth and equable in the roughest weather." Washington Irving

"The old man laughed loud and joyously, shook up the details of his anatomy from head to foot, and ended up by saying such a laugh was money in a man's pocket, because it cut down the doctor's bills like anything." Mark Twain

A sense of humor is too important to leave to chance. Keep a videotape of your favorite comedies and watch them when you need a lift. Keep a photo album of your favorite anecdotes and comics; share your humor with your family and friends.

"A good laugh is sunshine in a house." William Thackeray

"A key to keeping a sense of humor in a family is always remembering no matter how miserable your relationships are with each other, it could be worse. I get a lot of reaction on the mother/daughter relationship from people, and people seem so surprised that there are other mothers and daughters who share that antagonism and love at the same time. Many mothers and daughters have written and said for a while their only communica-

45

Having fun in your teenage years is part of life; you are creating lifelong memories you will never forget. Keep many of those memories laced with laughter. Promise never to let it be a crime to have fun in your life. **Always keep an air of playfulness, taking time to laugh and smile daily.** Let there be laughter, and let it start with you.

"...Parsons, even in his prosperity, always fretting; Potts, in the midst of his poverty, ever laughing. It seems, then, that happiness in this life rather depends on internals than externals...." Benjamin Franklin

6

Be Able to Speak Up But Avoid Talking Back

"A Mule makes no headway while he's kicking." E. C. McKenzie

"I can't believe you won't let me go! I'm speechless!" **"If only you could stay that way!"** *Anonymous*

"Young men have a passion for regarding their elders as senile." Henry Adams

"Children today are tyrants. They contradict their parents, gobble their food, and tyrannize their teachers." Socrates

Parents and teens have always had their share of disagreements. They will continue to have them as long as parents and teens coexist under one roof. This is not a lecture about having to agree with everything your parents say; that would be inhuman. It's not about suppressing your feelings either. On the contrary, **it's important for you to express even your strongest feelings to your parents.** It won't always be easy for your parents to hear what you have to say, but give them a chance. Most will try to respond quietly and thoughtfully to even harsh criticism. Many could accept you saying, "I'm really upset. I felt embarrassed when you criticized me in front of my friends!" That's a genuine expression of your frustration. They will try to understand. Few will accept without a

47

strong response the statement, "You're so (BLEEP)! Why don't you just go to (BLEEP)!"

"Question authority, but raise your hand first." Bob Thaves

"Anger is a wind which blows out the lamp of the mind." Anonymous

All teenagers get angry at their parents. No one ever promised there wouldn't be a few rocky moments for even the best families. **Just don't let the rocks turn into boulders. Even strong feelings do not excuse hateful comments by either you or your parents.** You'll find that even though they're frequently upset about things you do, they never tell you they hate you, and they won't permit you to talk that way to them without a strong reaction. Hate breeds hate in return; it's that simple.

"Do not speak unless you can improve the silence." Edmund Muskie

"A gentle answer turns away wrath, but a harsh word stirs up anger." Proverbs 15:1

Sometimes when you feel you're going to say something you'll regret, take seriously the old suggestion, "count to ten before you speak." It works. Take time to get out of the situation; go to your room **before** you're sent there. Taking distance doesn't show weakness; it shows wisdom. Let your parents know what you're doing, "Look, I don't want to say anything I'll regret. Can I go to my room for a few minutes to calm down and think? I'll talk to you, but let me think it through for a few minutes." Once in your room, count to ten, take a few deep breaths, and then think about what you want to say. If you are still struggling with strong feelings, try writing some of your thoughts and feelings on paper or call a friend to talk about how to handle the problem. **Writing and talking will help you control your emotions and help you give a better message when you do talk to your parents. Make sure you come back to talk the problem through.** Most parents will try to give you the distance and time you need, but they want to make sure they don't avoid important conversations. Keep in mind, when you're taking time, parents also get some time to cool down. You'll have more luck getting through to your parents when they're calm than when they're in a shouting match with you.

"A closed mouth catches no flies." French Proverb

"I have never been hurt by anything I didn't say." Calvin Coolidge

When you do go back to talk, there are a few things to keep in mind. Try avoiding words like "everyone else," "It's all your fault," "It's not fair!" **Avoid bringing up other parents; you have your parents as parents, not anyone else. Use your head in choosing good words that build a case for your position.** Don't talk about blame, talk about what both you and your parents can do in the future to take care of the problem. Since you have a mind of your own, use it to help find a workable solution.

"You raise your voice when you should reinforce your argument."
Samuel Johnson

"When you lose your temper--you really lose something. You lose the ability to think sanely and to make balanced decisions."
George Sweeting

In minor disagreements don't try to make a federal case out of every disagreement. **There will be times that you and your parents will see things very differently, but people can learn to agree to disagree.** It takes two to argue.

If one fighter steps out of the match, there is no fight. Instead of bristling at advice parents give, learn to let go of the struggle to make them see your side. You can remain privately convinced that you are right and still support the right of both sides to disagree and express their point of view. Try saying a simple statement, "I guess we don't see eye to eye on this, but thanks for the suggestion, Dad. I'll have to think some more about it."

"But curb thou the high spirit in thy breast,
For gentle ways are best, and keep aloof
from sharp contentions." Homer, The Illiad

Most parents would agree that it's not always the teen's fault when things go bad. Parents have to work at listening and communicating carefully as well. **If your parents fail to listen or are just plain wrong, don't try to force them to admit it in the heat of battle.** Such teen tactics seldom work. Give your parents the time and distance they need to calm down. Most will come back to admit their mistakes and correct them.

"Everyone should be quick to listen, slow to speak, and slow to become angry." James 1:19

You're free to say anything you wish to your parents, even if those feelings are not pleasant. But if you want to get through to them, just try to avoid screaming and calling them names. They just may try to do the same with you.

"This is a difficult period in our lives as we start to cross the thin line between adolescence and adulthood. We often think our parents don't understand. We need to remember that they were teenagers once, and they survived. They are willing to lend their experiences to help us survive." Malcolm-Jamal Warner, Theo on "The Bill Cosby Show"

7

Speak the Truth

"I have done extensive fieldwork with five children and can tell you as scientific fact that the only time they tell the truth is when they are in pain." Bill Cosby

"So you want a job, eh? Do you ever tell lies?" "No sir, but I can learn." Anonymous

"You can fool some of the people all of the time, and all of the people some of the time, but you cannot fool all of the people all of the time." Abraham Lincoln

"I didn't do it, and I won't do it again." Louis Armstrong

Think of your best friends. Do you trust them? Sure you do, or they wouldn't be your friends. **You don't need a lecture on telling the truth, because you know how it feels to have someone not keep their word.** For some "I promise I won't tell," really means, "I won't tell until I can find someone to listen." "I'll pay you back," means "You'll see your money if I win the lottery." You don't like it when friends lie to you. Does that help you understand why it is so important to your parents that you tell the truth.

"The will to truth is merely the longing for a stable world." Nietzsche

"The liar's punishment is not in the least that he is not believed, but that he cannot believe anyone else." George Bernard Shaw

"No man has a good enough memory to make a successful liar."
Lincoln

Saying something that you know isn't true or covering up the truth are both lying. **There are only two ways of dealing with people, to be trustworthy or not to be trustworthy.**

"Every violation of truth is not only a sort of suicide in the liar, but is a stab at the health of human society." Ralph Waldo Emerson

"No pillow is as soft as a clear conscience." John Wooden, UCLA

It's not easy to stand for telling the truth in our society. There are too many excuses that make it easy for people to take the easy way out. Have you heard any of these statements to defend lying? "Everything is relative;" "Everyone does it;" "The truth will only hurt;" "What they don't know won't hurt them." Add to these the attitude that seems very prevalent today with teens and some adults--that it's OK to lie, if you can get away with it. Some teens say, "Parents aren't friends--their parents. You're supposed to lie to parents! It's in the movies!" But parents are people too! **You and your parents are in this together for the long haul whether you like it or not.** Many of your friends in high school will move out of your life; your parents will be with you for a lifetime.

You wouldn't sell out a friend. Don't sell parents out either. The momentary opportunity you may enjoy will never make up for the trust a lie can destroy. It takes a history to build trust; it takes only one lie to kill it for months. If you sneak around, you make parents become detectives. If they can't trust your words, you make them demand proof. If you don't face the music, they'll make the music louder when they find out. That's no way for any family to live. Honesty may be painful at times, but it's never destructive.

> *"Character is much easier kept than recovered."* Thomas Paine

> *"If you tell the truth, you don't have to remember anything."* Mark Twain

It's not "cool" to lie, and it's not right. The world tries to make everything relative, but there are some things that are just plain wrong. Lying over things that are essential moral issues is one of them. Sure, you can enjoy an occasional bluff in a card game or a practical joke with a friend. Enjoying April Fool's Day is not a sin. **In the game of life there are "lies" that are fun only because they are exceptions coming from a context of trust.** Practical jokes don't work unless the "victim" expects you to be truthful.

> *"Delusions, errors, and lies are like huge, gaudy vessels, the rafters of which are rotten and worm-eaten, and those who embark in them are fated to be shipwrecked."* Buddha

> *"Shall I tell you...to buy friendship through cheating?...No! For unless you are honest in small matters, you won't be in large ones. If you cheat even a little, you won't be honest with greater responsibilities."* Luke 16:9-10

What about "white lies?" Before you falsify, misrepresent or otherwise disguise the truth to protect, to shield from pain, or harmlessly comfort another, make sure that if others ever found out most would accept your reasons. If that is not the case and you would be embarrassed for others to find out, you are probably kidding yourself. Pursue truth whenever and wherever important commitments are involved. Stand your ground, even when no one else seems to be with you. **Be known for the promises you keep, not for the ones you have broken.**

"In matters of principle, stand like a rock; in matters of taste, swim with the current." Thomas Jefferson

"Integrity is the glue that holds our way of life together." Rev. Billy Graham

"But I've already told so many lies! Why read on?" You're not alone; most of us have had to learn the hard way that truth is the best course to take. **It's never too late to build an honest future starting today.** It starts with the gift of forgiveness and moves to a new commitment to change.

"If we confess our sins, he is faithful and just to forgive us our sins, and to cleanse us from all unrighteousness." 1 John 1:9

No matter what your past or what you end up doing with your life, your character can be an asset that all will respect. It is a fragile, but invaluable treasure. Treat it that way. **Be known as a "promise keeper", and that trait alone will assure your success in any career you choose.** People want to work with people they can count on.

"Truth is its own reward." Plato

"This, above all, to thine own self be true, and it must follow as the night the day, thou canst not then be false to any man." William Shakespeare

"Integrity has no need of rules." Albert Camus

As for your parents, they want to trust you. They want to know that when you tell them something, they can count on it being true. Most parents will do their best to be honest with you and maintain your trust. We have all seen too many parents and teens that don't trust each other. Once they lose that trust, it takes a long time to gain it back. Do your part, so that doesn't happen in your home.

"Stop lying to each other; tell the truth, for we are all parts of each other and when we lie to each other we are hurting ourselves." Ephesians 4:25

"Honesty and openness make you vulnerable. Be honest and open anyway." Jennifer James

8

Save Sex or Safe Sex

"This girl doesn't understand. This boy is fifteen years old. At fifteen years old, a boy will hit on a snake." The Bill Cosby Show

Saving sex for marriage didn't make it to the top or even the middle of the teen list for favorite values to live by. Taking precautions before having sex did. The decision to have sex outside of marriage is too important a choice to explore only one side of the issue. This life lesson is the longest in the book, but it's worth reading from beginning to end. It's one of the more important choices facing you as a teen--save sex or safe sex.

"Everybody does it"/"Then you won't have trouble finding someone else to do it with." Sol Gordon

"If a man asks you to do something funny to him, I want you to give me your word of honor that you'll run screaming into the night." Florence King's mother

A case can be made for saving sex for marriage. Sex is not dirty, and it's not evil. Sexual intercourse is a powerful, sensual, and spiritual experience that is wonderful in the right context. Even in the wrong context, experimenting sexually can be exciting, but it can also develop a habit that is costly to you and to others.

"You can't get a little bit pregnant." Anonymous

Having sex before marriage may not make warts grow, drive you crazy with guilt, or turn you into a slut. We're also not suggesting your feelings for the opposite sex are no more than a set of glands calling to a matching pair. You can and will feel strong affection for many you date. **But having intercourse outside of marriage is not a simple decision.**

"Sexual sophistication without sexual responsibility is sexual disaster!" Dr. James Dobson

"When kids are empowered with information and stimulated by hope for the future, it has a contraceptive effect. Education. Employment. Their own bank accounts. Good health. Family involvement. Self-esteem. These are all contraceptives. We have a message that delaying sexual activity is good...for the long haul." Michael Carrera

Many people in America have made the decision to do significantly more than just sleep together before marriage. They have had sex, and, admittedly, most have survived. By their actions they were living out the 'ethic of intimacy'. They are acting out the belief that if two people love each other and are serious about the relationship, there is nothing wrong with having intercourse. Unfortunately, in practice, that usually means individuals will have a series of sexual partners, because many close relationships will break up. You will go through many changes in your teen and young adult years. What you want from your 'Mr./Mrs. Right' will change as well. **You may fall in love many times in your life, and yet nothing binds those relationships together but feelings.** If surveys are correct, many will settle down with one person, live together intimately for a time, and then get married. Is having sex with all the people you are "serious about" the best way to experience sex? We don't think so. The more people you have sexual intimacy with before marriage, the harder it is to make intimacy in marriage special. **If marriage means less, it offers less. When you give sex freely, what do you give when it is special?**

"Why buy the cow, when you can get the milk for free?" American Proverb

"Avoid sexual looseness like the plague! Every other sin that a man commits is done outside his own body, but this is an offense against his own body. Have you forgotten that your body is the temple of the Holy Spirit, who lives in you and is God's gift to you, and that you are not the owner of you own body? You have been bought, and at what a price! Therefore bring glory to God in your body." I Corinthians 6:18-20

We feel sex before marriage is wrong, if for no other reason than it is not the best way to experience sex. Saving intercourse for marriage gives your complete commitment the best of all possible beginnings for your sexual experience. With commitment you have your life together to make sex work for your relationship.

You may agree, but it does not change the fact that sex remains a very big deal in our society. **The choice to have sex will never be far away. It is a choice you will have to make many times throughout your teen years.** If you need reasons to wait, try any of these on for size: "You don't want to"; "You're not ready"; "You want to wait until you are married"; "You're not using birth control." It may help you to know that millions of others your age feel the same way you do and have decided not to have sex before marriage.

"Deciding your own values should be a personal decision and not influenced by others. It is important to know these values, and the limits that go with them, and to not let others persuade us into doing or believing things we may not be comfortable with. Peer pressure is a strong influence, but our peers are not the ones who take the consequences for our actions--we are. We need to prepare our limits.... Thinking in advance about how we feel and what we would say can reduce the awkwardness of the situation when we actually face it." Gretchen Davis, college student

When someone says you are "not normal," you can reply with conviction, "I never asked to be average." If someone says, "You would if you really loved me," you can be sure that's only a line--really loving a person is not proved by having sex. Having sex will not make you a "real man"--All it proves is that the man can ejaculate. Having a baby will not make a girl a "real woman"--There are plenty of "real women" who have lived feminine, fulfilled lives without ever having a baby. **Having sex will not cure loneliness, and it will not make you popular for the right reasons.**

"Saying 'no' can be a gift of freedom." Anonymous Poster

"Putting out will not win you popularity. It will only get you a bad reputation; because no matter what a guy says, he will talk about you afterward to other guys. I didn't put out, and I was popular. I was the editor of our high school paper, on the debate team, a cheerleader and vice president of our graduating class. Sure, there were guys who tried to score with me, but when they knew they couldn't, they respected me and remained my friends anyway." A Young Woman from Little Rock

Young men, don't buy or perpetuate the male myth-- "Women want to be pushed, or, more commonly, 'No' really means 'Yes'!" **Any forcible sex is rape! The choice to have sex is something no one should force.** In a country where eroticized violence is depicted in one out of every eight movies, it is not hard to find inappropriate role models for what it's like for a man to "take sex from a woman." Men do not seem satisfied to leave such scenes to the movies; every six minutes a woman is raped in the United States. From the age a young girl first walks home alone from school, she learns to check her shadow, shun certain streets, listen for footsteps. It's an intense fear that every woman at some time will come to know. It's a shame that any woman should have to fear men. **Pushing sex on an unwilling partner is not a parlor game; it's a crime.** Don't let your actions add to that fear.

Young women, don't count on the morals of your date. Avoid drinking too much or dressing provocatively with dates you don't know or trust. If you leave your keys in your car, it is still theft if someone takes it. It still isn't smart. If you make it easy to lose control, it is still rape, but don't increase the odds.

Don't wait for passion to make the choice for you. If you decide to abstain, keep your relationships in control. You may want to take out "party insurance"; practice safe party and date tactics. Until you know a date well, plan for a safe date. Arrange to have a friend at a party that you can ride home with. If you have a good friend you trust, double date to have someone to help keep things in control.

> *"You are not weird (for saying no to sex); you are unusual. But the best always is. Be true to yourself. Some men still appreciate the obvious goodness you possess. It does not take experience to know that having sex is no substitute for making love." Anonymous 22 year-old college senior*

"Can't I do *anything*?" you might be asking. Total "sexual" abstinence is unrealistic and not necessarily wise. Caring

61

for someone sexually is more than having intercourse. Holding, cuddling, caressing, and kissing are other forms

of closeness that are often more sensual and exciting than genital union. **You can be close while still saying "no" to intercourse.** Just remember that what you know about sexual physiology will not inhibit sexual activity any more than understanding the digestive process will help you control your eating. If you decide in favor of sexual responsibility, you will have to live out that decision in your relationships.

"Freedom is not procured by a full enjoyment of what is desired, but by controlling the desire." Epictetus

"Nobody's ever died from not having sex. It's the one appetite that's not necessary to fulfill." Kathleen Sullivan, Project Respect

Sex isn't dirty; it's a beautiful God given gift. Make the choice to keep it that way. Also learn to keep dating and sex in perspective. **Many young men and women will prove to be far better at sustaining a loving relationship over time than they are at dating or having sex on demand with a stranger they hardly know.** Give love and commitment a chance; your time for fulfilling sex will follow.

> *"A Young man threatens to give you up because you do not allow petting and kissing. Figure it this way--the more you refuse, the more anxious he becomes; the more anxious he becomes, the more he sees you; the more he sees you the better you have of showing him your true sweet nature--and then, well, maybe he will be your husband and have the right to pet and kiss you." Sara Swain--"An authority on the affairs of the heart", 1925*

> *"The best contraceptive is the word no--repeated frequently." Margaret Smith*

The message you hear most from parents about sex can be summed up in three words--"don't," "stop," and "no." There are reasons they give that message--when teenagers have sex before adulthood young people are often too vulnerable and too easily exploited. **But living up to that message doesn't always work; that leaves parents with an uncomfortable but necessary double message--"Don't do it, but if you're going to have sex anyway, use precautions to make it as safe as possible."**

> *"Teenage boys are willing to discuss birth control with their girlfriends...but nearly one in four thinks the best time to do it is after sex." Survey by the Salvation Army Booth Memorial Center in Oakland, CA*

> *"You can't look into the eyes of someone you love and tell if they have the virus." Dr. Karen Hein*

"Would you be more careful if it was you that got pregnant?"
Advertisement in birth control for men

"We all know there's that other thing out there. Which means we all have to use a little condom sense. A prophylactic, from the Latin prophylactorum, which means: strange party favors. I know you hate to put it on. In the heat of passion you don't want to say, 'Let's stop and put on a balloon.'" Robin Williams

Most sexually active teenagers don't use birth control or contraceptives the first time they have intercourse. Unfortunately, all it takes is one time you don't use birth control for a pregnancy to result.

"Don't make a baby if you can't be a father." National Urban League

"If you cannot be chaste, be cautious." Spanish Proverb

"A real man offers protection instead of temptation." Sana Swain, 1925

At some time, in the next ten years it is pretty likely that you will be tempted to get involved with sex. **If you decide to have sex, you don't have to have that decision result in an unwanted child or a sexually transmitted disease.** But to take advantage of protection, birth control must be planned for.

"But they don't make rubbers in my size! Don't be fooled. Condoms are manufactured in one size which will fit all men, regardless of individual differences. If you douche or urinate right after sex, you won't get pregnant! Don't be fooled. Sperm travels to the uterus within seconds. Once there, jumping up and down, douching, or urinating will not prevent them from moving to the egg in the fallopian tubes. I can't get pregnant the first time! Don't be fooled. Pregnancy can be the result whenever you have intercourse and don't use birth control--the first time, or any time. In fact, over

64

a period of a year, about 80% of those not using birth control do get pregnant." Planned Parenthood Brochure

If you are entertaining the idea of being sexually active or plan on trying it "just once," have an available means of birth control in your possession for use at the appropriate time. Just as having a seat belt does not mean we condone driving recklessly. Having birth control protection does not mean we suggest having intercourse before marriage. You already know how most parents feel about that. Not everyone chooses to have sex before marriage. Many wait for marriage, and so can you.

"Kids feel AIDS just can't happen to them just like girls feel pregnancy cannot happen to them. This is a characteristic attitude in adolescence when kids feel invulnerable and omnipotent. It's as if they are saying, 'You can't prepare for lightning and love is like lightning. If it hits you, you aren't responsible.'" Pamela Cantor

If you do try to use protection, don't expect every partner to welcome its use. With condoms, some protest--"Don't you take the pill!" or "Do you have something I can catch?" Stand your ground! Try soft power by saying, "Let's try it once. If you don't like it, we can think about doing something else." Don't be bullied. Care about your partner, but don't fail to protect yourself or your future. Let's face it, if you're too embarrassed to buy condoms, you are not ready to take on the responsibility of having sex with a partner. **Besides, no sexual experience is worth dying for.** Unfortunately for teenagers, the AIDS virus does not forgive. At this point, infection with the virus is a curse that will last until death. If you choose to have sex, by planning for intercourse you can at least take minimal responsibility for being sexually active.

"...Sexually active teenagers will be the next AIDS 'high risk' group." Newsweek

"When you go to bed with one man, you go to bed with his entire sexual history, and the history of all his sexual partners." Ellen Goodman

"So the message of the 1980's and the 1990's must be: Practice no sex that could spread AIDS. If you are sexually active and either you or your partner could be infected, use a (latex) condom and a spermicide properly all the time." Dr. Neil R. Schram, internist, and former chairman of the Los Angeles City/County AIDS Task Force

This is not to imply that any approach will provide fail-safe protection, but, except for abstinence, using condoms consistently and continuously with all partners is the best protection you have. Though by no means perfect, latex condoms have been found to provide an effective barrier against AIDS, syphilis, gonorrhea, chlamydia, and the herpes virus. It may also ward off human papilloma virus (HPV), implicated in genital warts and cervical cancer. And, of course, condoms help prevent unwanted pregnancy. Most parents would want to be very clear about how strongly they feel about delaying sexual involvement until marriage. But if you choose to have sex, be responsible for protecting you and your partner from an unwanted pregnancy or sexually transmitted disease.

"This love of which I speak is slow to lose patience. It looks for a way of being constructive. It is not possessive: it is neither anxious to impress nor does it cherish inflated ideas of its own importance. Love has good manners and does not pursue selfish advantage." I Corinthians 13:4-5

Most parents want you to know you can come to them to talk about sexual matters. They may be upset with you at times, but most will work with you because they love you. Few parents want to hear your "True Confessions" after every date, but they do want to help you face any sexual problem or concerns you might have. **If you find it hard to talk to your parents, find some adult you trust and respect from church or school. Go ahead and risk talking to someone.** The choice is still yours--save sex or safe sex.

"Even more important than finding the right mate is being the right mate." Anonymous

National HIV & AIDS Information and Referral Service 800-342-2437
V.D.(Venereal Diseases) National Hotline 800-227-8922

9

Treat Others as You Want to Be Treated

"When you're younger, you want to be sure that by the time you're 80 years old you can sit on the bench and look back and say, 'Man, I did it all. I didn't miss a thing.' What you never meant to do was to hurt anyone, but then you see the look on the face of the person you didn't mean to hurt, and then you realize that what you stand to lose is worth so much more...." Bill Cosby

There is probably no more important lesson in life than the one expressed in the Golden Rule: **"Do unto others as you would have them do unto you."** Even modern day studies on ethics often seem to come down to this all important lesson.

"What you do not want others to do to you, do not do to others." Confucius

"Whatever is hateful unto thee, do it not unto thy fellow: this is the whole Torah; the rest is explanation." Rabbi Hillel

Relationships are like bank deposit systems. If you don't put anything positive into a relationship, you tend to get nothing back. When you open a bank account and start writing checks, a very quick message comes back to you when you run out of funds--"El Bounce-o!" Banks can be heartless. The same is true with life. People who don't treat others with empathy and caring should not be surprised when the world shows no concern in return. The "Me Generation" is more than just "looking out for #1." The "Me Generation" expects *others* to look out for them when they don't give anything back in return.

> *"If all you want is to make money, you go for the sure bet. But what about doing something for your fellow man? I'm not ambitious in the sense of wanting to be famous and make a lot of money. If you are, you're going to get kicked around a lot. Hollywood is notorious for that. They're going to make you pay. But if you want to make it in order to bring something into it, then they can't touch you."*
> *Actress Theresa Russell*

> *"The value of a man....should be seen in what he gives and not in what he is able to receive." Albert Einstein*

There's a Christian song that inspires many, entitled "You're The Only Jesus Some Will Ever See." Few of us seem to act that way. It's as if we say to ourselves, "Let the ones with wealth do it! We pay our taxes! That ought to be enough to take care of the problems in our society." Once we run out of people to blame, we take a turn at blaming God. After all, if God is so all powerful, how can he let people suffer? The stark reality remains the same; the "It's not my job!" attitude isn't going to get the job done in this changing, challenging world. **God needs all of us doing our job, and that includes you.**

> *"We make a living by what we get, but we make a life by what we give." Winston Churchill*

> *"When you are good to others, you are best to yourself." Benjamin Franklin*

You can make a difference. Living by the Golden Rule means going out of your way to help people in ways you would want to be helped. It means trying to understand why people do things instead of just reacting to what they do. It means putting yourself in their position, not just

demanding that they understand yours. **It means asking the question, "How would I feel if someone did that to me?"**

"If the world were a village of 1000 inhabitants, 700 would be non-white, 300 would be white. 300 of them would be Christians. 60 people would own half the total wealth. 500 would not have enough to eat. 600 would live in slums. 700 would be illiterate. If this were our village, we would want it to change. But in fact this

is our village, for this is the world." From "Guiding," United Kingdom Girl Guide Periodical

"Do not do unto others as you would that they should do unto you. Their tastes may not be the same." George Bernard Shaw

"We can do no great things; only small things with great love." Mother Teresa

Some days you may get taken for granted. You may even be abused for your caring, but do it anyway. There is more personal satisfaction in "being" a caring person than there is in just "trying" to be nice. Even when it doesn't seem to be appreciated, others will see your efforts. There is no more valuable reputation you can have than to be known as a person who cares. There may be times you run out of money, but you won't run out of deposits in your "people account."

"There are different ways of knowing. The power of those core statements (of the Golden Rule), the fact that they survived, derives, I would guess, from the fact that they tap into a core truth of human nature--or biology. Jesus, Confucius, Buddha, Hillel, and the others somehow knew the same thing that we can now begin to know from research that pinpoints hostility and anger as such powerful killers of people. The flip side is that being kind and gentle and considerate, expecting the best from others and treating others with consideration, keeps people alive." Dr. Redford Williams

"Give and it will be given to you. A good measure, pressed down, shaken together, and running over will be poured into your lap." Luke 6:38

A wise parent summed it up this way, **"The best way to have a friend is to be a good friend to others. The best way to feel special is to make others feel important."** We might add that the best insurance you will ever buy will be the goodwill you generate in your daily dealings with the people you meet. "Treat all as you wish to be treated" is a simple but important secret of life everyone needs to live by.

"I am of the opinion that my life belongs to the whole community, and as long as I live, it is my privilege to do for it what I can. I want to be thoroughly used up when I die, for the harder I work, the more I live. I rejoice in life for its own sake. Life is no brief candle to me--it's a sort of splendid torch which I've got a hold of for the moment and I want to make it burn as brightly as possible before handing it on to future generations." George Bernard Shaw

"The service we render to others is really the rent we pay for our room on this earth." Sir Wilfred Grenfell

10

Learn to Work with People You Do Not Like

"We have met the enemy and they are us." Pogo

"Hating people is like burning down your own house to get rid of a rat." Harry Emerson Fosdick

"It is the human race that is the only animal that blushes, or needs to. You just have to remember they were made at the end of the week's work. " Mark Twain

One of the easiest things to learn in this world is to hate. Unfortunately, **the world cries out for peace, and that requires people who have learned how to be hard to hate.** It's not difficult to make an enemy. All you need is to meet a person on the rocky side of their character. First impressions are hard to change. When a child touches a hot plate, few children give the oven a second chance to be "nice". They avoid it like the plague. That's what we do with our "enemies." We set up what some affectionately call "mafia pacts--You don't bother me too much, I don't bother you!" Before you are quick to say, "They deserve it," take a look at your own track record. Have you ever had a day you've been other than "Mr/Ms. Sunshine?" If you're honest with yourself, that's an easy one to answer. Give others you meet the benefit of the doubt that you would hope they would give you. Maybe they were having a bad day when you met them. One of the rules for becoming a "peace maker" is to give people a chance to grow on you instead of looking for reasons to hate them.

"Though one should in battle conquer a thousand men, he who conquers himself has a more glorious victory." Buddha

"I will not permit any man to narrow my soul by making me hate him." Booker T. Washington

"When the man's ways are pleasing to the Lord, he makes even his enemies live at peace with him." Proverbs 16:7

Having a bad early experience is not the only way we make enemies. Sometimes we are turned off by what we fear or don't know. **Everybody has grown up with some biases, but you can learn to look and live beyond them.** Don't let age, gender, religion, race, job, wealth, job status, or nationality confuse the facts. All people are people! With biases we have preconceived ideas, we keep our distance and then look for evidence to prove what we fear. That's why biases are hard to change. All you have to do is watch the news, and you can find evidence to support any bias-- "All those people are the same. They're all criminals!" Unfortunately, only criminals seem to make the news. Since all groups have their share of criminals, it's not hard to keep our biases strong.

"People who fight fire with fire usually end up with ashes." Abigail Van Buren

"Both read the same Bible, and pray to the same God; and each invokes his aid against the other. It may seem strange that any men should dare to ask a just God's assistance in wringing their bread from the sweat of other men's faces; but let us judge not, that we be not judged. The prayers of both could not be answered--that of

neither has been answered fully. With malice toward none; with charity for all; with firmness in the right, as God gives us to see the right, let us strive on to finish the work we are in; to bind up the nation's wounds...to do all which may achieve and cherish a just and lasting peace among ourselves, and with all nations."
Abraham Lincoln

"Before you start on the road of revenge, dig two graves." Chinese Proverb

Be different! Don't look for enemies when you can learn to make friends. Life is not all roses; you will have to be able to confront people. Learn to face issues instead of fighting people. Look for the best in people and you'll usually find it. Instead of avoiding your enemies, find ways to spend time with them. Talk to them about some of their interests at breaks or lunch. Ask for their help on something they do well. Instead of having your "face in park," smile at them in the hallways, even if they don't smile back. Find a way to work or play together whenever you can. Don't gossip; if you can't talk about the problem eyeball to eyeball, no one else needs to hear your complaints.

"There is a saying, 'Love your friends and hate your enemies.' But I say: 'Love your enemies! Pray for those who persecute you!' If you love only those who love you, what good is that? Even scoundrels do that much. If you are friendly only to your friends, how are you different from anyone else?" Matthew 6:43-44,46-47

"I don't like that man; I'm going to have to get to know him better."
Abraham Lincoln

"It is very hard to dislike someone you have helped." Benjamin Franklin

"Christ did not seek to overcome evil with evil. He overcame evil with good. Although crucified by hate, he responded with aggressive love." Martin Luther King, Jr.

When you act like an enemy, you'll probably find more than a few people who are willing to be an enemy back. **If you treat no man as an enemy, they'll have a hard time keeping their own hates and fears alive.** Don't expect quick changes. It takes a history to develop any positive trust with "enemies". Even if it doesn't work in changing

a relationship, you will have done what you can do to work for peace in your home, your neighborhood, your school, and at your place of work.

"Peace is not the absence of conflict, but the ability to cope with conflict by peaceful means." Ronald Reagan

"If you would win a man to your cause, first convince him that you are his true friend.. Therein is a drop of honey that catches his heart, which say what he will, is the greatest highroad to his reason,

and which once gained, you will find but little trouble in convincing his judgement of the justice of your cause, if indeed, that cause be really a just one." Abraham Lincoln

People with character don't try things. They decide how they want to be as a person and they live it, irrespective of what others do. It's easy to make enemies; it's noble work to make an enemy a friend. Work at peace in your family, at school, and in our world.

"Three months prior to my release, Said, one of my captors, said..., 'Do you forgive me?' to which I replied, 'Yes, Said. I do forgive you and ask your forgiveness too.' For there were times I was filled with anger and hate. And on the evening of my release, Haj (another captor), quoting from my letter home to my loved ones, said, 'Father, forgive them for they know not what they do.' I could not help but think these were the words of Jesus, who died in peace and returns to his disciples not with anger or retaliation against them, but with the simple greeting of 'Peace be with you.'" The Rev. Lawrence Jenco, former hostage in Lebanon

"People are unreasonable, illogical, and self-centered. Love them anyway." Jennifer James

11

Be Courteous to Other People

"Parents are not just interested in justice; they want quiet." Bill Cosby

"I don't want to panic anybody, but three million electric guitars and amplifiers were given out as Christmas presents last year. This could be the end of eardrums as we know them!" Robert Orben

"Nothing separates the generations more than music. By the time a child is eight or nine, he has developed a passion for his own music that is even stronger than his passions for procrastination and weird clothes." Bill Cosby

Being courteous with others is not just something that you ought to leave to the Boy Scouts and the Girl Scouts of the world. It's something that makes relationships work no matter who you are. **One of the hardest things to learn in ones journey from childhood into adulthood is that the world does not revolve around your needs.** Just because many teens enjoy loud music, does not mean that others share the same tastes in music. While their "Ghetto Blaster" fills the air with music others may consider noise, they scurry for cover with scowls on their faces. Just because you want to go to the mall, does not mean that parents have the time or the inclination to take you. The world isn't your private playground; other people share the space.

We're not sure "common courtesy" is a good phrase. If it was that "common," you wouldn't think we would have to train so many teens to use it. We must confess, not even all adults show evidence of having learned any such lecture. Many adults you meet will **not** be polite. In fact, sometimes rudeness will seem to pay. **Rude people often enjoy short-term results as others give in to avoid having to deal with such people. But they pay in other ways; much of their life is spent alone.** It makes no difference what others do; most parents expect their teens to be courteous. If you learn this lesson now, you will be pleasantly surprised that being courteous will work for you throughout life. If that's too long to wait to see a benefit, being courteous is a sure winner with any date.

Work with other family members to set a volume level for your radio and stereo that is acceptable to all concerned. Try keeping your door closed or using a headset. Most parents might just as well try playing by the same rules; some of their music may not thrill you either.

> *"Amplification not only destroys the purity of sound, it also damages the ear, so that in time the ear is incapable of making distinctions.... Loudness, like smog and toxic wastes, is a destructive product of our technology." Jack Smith*

> *"Politeness goes far, yet costs nothing." Samuel Smiles*

Being courteous and polite is not limited to how loud you play your music. It has to do with an attitude of concern for the feelings and sensitivities of others. The list is

sometimes comical, but not any less important: Put the toilet seat down and flush before leaving; clean up the crumbs after you snack; put your dirty clothes in the hamper; be tactful instead of blunt; open doors for others; and, of course, take time to say "thank you," "please," and "I'm sorry." You could add to the list yourself.

"Introducing yourself to others, shaking their hands and making eye contact are all part of being polite and letting others know that you are interested." Dr. Philip G. Zimbardo and Shirley Radl

"Politeness is the chief sign of culture." Baltasar Gracian

"Politeness has been well defined as benevolence in small things." Thomas Macaulay

Looking out for the needs and feelings of others is a sign of maturity. There is something in it for you as well; your courtesy will breed courtesy in return. Some have called it "benevolent self-interest"--looking out for the needs of others makes it more likely that others will return the favor. That's a true win-win arrangement. Try to make it a reality in your home.

"A spoonful of honey will catch more flies than a gallon of vinegar." Benjamin Franklin

"The words of a wise man's mouth are gracious." Ecclesiastes 10:12

"The greater man the greater courtesy." Lord Tennyson

81

12

Practice Makes Closer to Perfect

"Never try and teach a pig to sing. He can't sing, and it irritates the pig." Anonymous

"Apathy can be learned. All you have to do is relax a little harder." Bob Orben

"Easy doesn't do it." Al Bernstein

"There is no such thing as a free lunch." Anonymous

Anything worthwhile in life is going to take work and effort. Unfortunately, most teenagers live in a world that builds an illusion that life is easy. In movies, even the toughest problems are finished in two hours; on television, they can stretch it out to a mini-series. People, young and old, spend hundreds of dollars on lotteries to become instant millionaires. One cartoon went so far at to show a teen marching with a timely placard that read, "Instant Gratification Isn't Fast Enough." With that kind of programming it's not too surprising that many teens think that life's victories can be won at the snap of their fingers. They want to buy a surfboard and visualize riding the eight footers with cameras rolling. After three hours of failing to find that elusive "sweet spot" and falling into the ocean, the board stays in the garage. That musical instrument that sounds so beautiful in the hands of a skilled musician, somehow doesn't work the same way when you buy your own and try to play it. The truth is--it doesn't play itself. It requires fingers honed by hours of practice, fingers that now move effortlessly across the keys. **Excellence seldom comes from miracles; it takes work.**

"Practice doesn't make you perfect. Practice makes you better. Nothing makes you perfect." Bobby Orr

"Everyone has a will to win, but very few have the will to prepare to win." Vince Lombardi

Stop searching for a magic wand. **The key to success echoes through three simple words--practice, practice, practice.** Important victories in every area are won on the practice field first. Even with practice, you will never win them all,

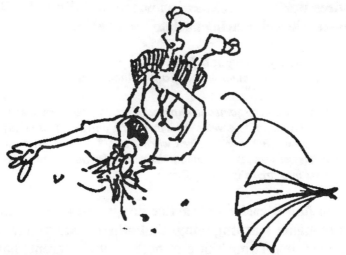

but you will increase your batting average. They pay a .300 hitter more than they pay a .200 hitter, but you don't get that kind of average by sitting on the couch watching TV.

Victories in the real world come to the doers not the observers.

"Talent is only the start. You must keep working your talent." Irving Berlin

"Genius is 1 percent inspiration and 99 percent perspiration." Thomas Alva Edison

Life is a never ending journey, a series of challenges where we learn through practice to reach mastery in one area, only to move on to the next challenge. Early on, taking two steps on your own was a victory; now you walk without thinking. You will learn how to drive, soon you'll swear you're driving on autopilot. You will never master everything, nor do you need to. Put your practice time into those things that are worth doing well. **Being good always requires work and awkward moments of failure, but the masters keep bouncing back to try it again.**

"Winners say, 'It may be difficult, but it's possible.' Losers say, 'It may be possible, but it's too difficult.'" Anonymous

"To me a winner is someone who recognizes his God-given talents, works his tail off to develop them into skills, and uses those skills to accomplish his goals. Even when I lost, I learned what my weaknesses were, and I went out the next day to turn those weaknesses into strengths." Larry Bird

You'll find it easier to practice things you want to learn and tougher learning things that others make you learn. You will learn your share of both, as your parents have. Drilling to master algebra may seem pointless at the time, but the discipline needed to achieve mastery in math will help you whenever you have to discipline your mind to solve a problem.

"Diligence is the mother of good luck" Benjamin Franklin

"Skill to do comes of doing." Ralph Waldo Emerson

One school in Hawaii requires every junior high student without medical limitations to run nine miles without stopping before graduating into high school. They increase their running mileage gradually so by the end of the year they all meet their goal and graduate. In high school, when student's say, "I can't do it," teachers reply, "That's what you said about running nine miles." Such time invested in learning self-discipline is never wasted.

"The waters wear the stones." Job 14:19

"Be prepared, or lose to someone who is." Sen. Bill Bradley

No matter how noble the goal, sustaining effort can be a real challenge. **If practice in one area becomes difficult, try rewarding yourself with an activity you enjoy.** Drill on your algebra you need to master to earn the chance to play an hour of basketball. By **earning** the basketball time working at your desk, taking those shots will be even more enjoyable.

"You got to make the deposits before you can enjoy the rewards. You got to study the lessons before you get the grades. You got to make the call before you get the sale. You got to learn the technique before you perfect the skill. You got to sweat on the practice field before you perform on the playing field." Zig Ziglar

"Stay away from any Christian who spends his days in laziness and does not follow the ideal of hard work we set up for you. Even while we were still there with you we gave you this rule: 'He who does not work shall not eat.'" 2 Thessalonians 3:4,10

Whatever the area, be prepared to work hard and the victories will be yours. Becoming a master at anything is never easy, but such ordeals make achievement what it is--a real accomplishment! You will soon find that when you master something, anything, it can be as sweet as a first love. Welcome to the challenge of finding the joy in mastery. May you find that joy throughout your life.

"Nothing in the world can take the place of persistence. Talent will not: nothing is more common than unsuccessful people with talent. Genius will not: unrewarded genius is almost a proverb. Education will not: the world is full of educated derelicts. Persistence and determination alone are omnipotent." Calvin Coolidge

13

Finish Work Early

"Man who sits with mouth open waiting for cooked goose to fly in, waits a long time." Chinese Proverb

"Between saying and doing many a pair of shoes is worn out." Italian Proverb

"Sometime seldom comes." Dr. Norman Vincent Peale

"What gets me out of bed in the morning? My mother." Anonymous Teenager

A wise old saying puts this lecture in perspective--**"If you have to swallow a frog, don't look at it too long!"** Easy to say, but it's not always easy to do.

Waiting for the "right time" to start things you hate doing is not a problem experienced only by teenagers. All of us are guilty of the same shortcoming at times. Just because many fall into the trap of letting work slide doesn't make it any less important to learn to stay ahead of your commitments. In fact, **the quicker you learn to develop a disciplined habit of starting work early, the sooner you experience the benefit.**

Know the number one enemy--yourself! You play the excuses in your head that help you avoid the discomfort of any unwanted task. You know what we're talking about.

Every time you even think about doing that English paper, your hand begins to shake as you reach for your book. Your brain searches for the best available excuse--"I haven't got time to get into it!" "It's not due for two weeks; I'll have more time this weekend." "I'm too tired; my brain cells are sapped!" "I forgot the book in my locker." "I work best under pressure; why even hassle it?" Have you played any of those excuse tapes? We've played them all, and then some. But we've learned to see them for what they are--excuses to avoid doing what needs to get done. Temporarily, they help short-circuit the pain; we leave the book on the desk and flip on the TV. We hide in the enjoyment of the noise until a parent or our conscience convicts us again--"You're doing it again! Turn that thing off and get started on that paper!" We go back and forth from the guilt of not doing the project to the discomfort of actually working on it.

"Never leave til tomorrow which you can do today." Benjamin
Franklin

"He slept beneath the moon,
He basked beneath the sun;
He lived a life of going-to-do
And died with nothing done."
James Albery

You know the struggle, but what can you do? Let's start with a little dose of reality we have all had to learn. **Rule #1: Not everything in life is fun or easy.** As a result, you can expect some discomfort in doing things that are hard and things that aren't fun. How does that help? Most of us have learned to avoid pain. Unfortunately, some painful activities in life still need to be done.

"Start by doing what's necessary, then what's possible and suddenly you are doing the impossible." St. Francis of Assisi

Rule #2: Most things are worse in anticipation than they are in reality. Mowing the lawn is never quite as bad as the pain of anticipating having to do it. Unless it's two acres with a push mower. In fact, getting any hated job done early can set you off on a positive roll--"Look what I did! This is going to be a good day!" It gives you a chance to blow the mind of your parent--"Martha, something's wrong with Jason! He mowed the lawn without being asked! He must be up to something!" **Avoided work weighs you down; timely progress gives you something to take pride in.** Which feeling do you want to have?

"Nothing is so fatiguing as the eternal hanging on of an uncompleted task." William James

"There's an old proverb..., 'Begin the thing and ye shall have the power. But those who do not begin, have not the power.'...If there are areas in your life where you put off needed action, these

unfulfilled tasks become a fatigue factor. They are like tiny leaks in your reservoirs of energy." Dr. Norman Vincent Peale

Anything without a date tends not to get done. **Try Rule #3: Anything worth doing is worth having a target date for completion.** Unfortunately, even with a target date, the further off the date, the easier it is to procrastinate. You know the argument--"I've got plenty of time!" Never settle for distant dreams; **successful people learn to have many target dates with short time goals along the way to completion.** You might say, "By the 15th of the month I'll finish the outline. By the first I should have the first-draft. That gives me a week for final changes."

"The lazier a man is, the more he plans to do tomorrow." Norwegian Proverb

Don't do the "whole load." You'd be unlikely to read a novel that didn't have chapter breaks to pace your reading. **Rule #4: Learn to break any project into small steps and get started on the first one within the first three days.** Even fifteen minutes of work can get the ball moving. Once moving, it's easier to keep it going.

"Get ahead of the problem and hit it; don't let it hit you first." Peter Ueberroth

"We cannot do everything at once, but we can do something at once." Calvin Coolidge

"Nothing is particularly hard if you divide it into small jobs." Henry Ford

Rule #5: Don't hide your plans, make commitments to friends or parents so you will have to do it. Privately held goals are easy to cheat on. When you tell others, you plan on working an hour on your term paper, they will remind you. That's not nagging, that's helping you do what you want done.

Rule #6: Never work so long on a project that you get sick of it. That's what happens when you cram. If you leave a project hating it, you'll have a hard time coming back to it. If you have put in a good hour of work, find a natural stopping point and take a break. Reward yourself with an activity you like--call a friend, shoot some baskets, take a ride, or watch a show. After the break, you'll be refreshed and look forward to getting back to work you were enjoying not dreading.

"Discipline is the process of scheduling the pain and pleasure of life in such a way as to enhance the pleasure by meeting and experiencing the pain first and getting it over with." M. Scott Peck, MD

All of life requires that people live and work smart. If you can learn to work ahead on important projects, you will have the time to enjoy being spontaneous. When you're behind on your work and friends ask you to join them for some fun activity, the procrastinators of the world often have to say, "Sorry, I've got too much work to do!" When you're ahead, you can say, "Sure! I'm caught up. Why not? Let's go!" If that sounds like a good deal to you, it's worth learning to work ahead on the things that matter at your school and in your home.

"When you procrastinate, do you produce your best effort? Let me suggest it was your only effort." Odette Pollar

14

Learn to Save Your Money for What's Important

"Did I hear you right? 'We are rich.' We're not rich. Your mother and I are rich. You are poor!" Bill Cosby Show

"'Dad, all my friends say I should have my own car,' the boy says earnestly one day. 'Wonderful, When are they going to buy it?'.... 'I'll tell you what: how's this for reasonable? Bring your friends over here and we'll have a collection, a matching funds collection. Whatever you get from them, I'll match it.'" Bill Cosby

"My father had an entitlement program: The day after we graduated he told us if we preferred to starve instead of work, we're entitled." Bob Orben

"If only God would give me some clear sign! Like making a large deposit in my name at a Swiss bank." Woody Allen

There is no more frustrating a topic for teens and parents than money. "We're not made of money!" "How much do your really **need**?" "When you have a job, you'll appreciate how much things cost!" "Do you think money grows on trees?" "Where's my change?" "You're all grown up now, you owe us $214,000."

"God gives the birds their food, but He does not throw it into their nests." Greek Proverb

"It's no use filling your pocket with money if you have got a hole in the corner." George Elliot

Don't act like a "five dollar millionaire." When you earn your "own money," resist the temptation to spend all you receive buying junk food, CD's, magazines, or clothes. Set aside some of what you earn to retire old debts and build new savings. Be your own money manager before you force your parents to take over the job.

"Dear Johnston (Lincoln's step-brother): Your request for eighty dollars I do not think it best to comply with now. At the various times when I have helped you a little you have said to me, 'We can get along very well now'; but in a very short time I find you in the same difficulty again. You are not lazy, and still you are an idler. You do not much dislike work, and still you do not work much, merely because it does not seem to you that you could get much for it. This habit of uselessly wasting time is the whole difficulty.... You are now in need of some money; and what I propose is, that you shall go to work, 'tooth and nail,' for somebody who will give you money for it. You have always been kind to me, and I do not mean to be unkind to you. On the contrary, if you will but follow my advice, you will find it worth more than eighty times eighty dollars to you." Abe Lincoln to John D. Johnston, January 2, 1851

The truth remains, you can't learn to handle money unless you have some to handle. That's why most teens receive an allowance and can get additional money for special work they do around the house. Whether in the home or on the job, most money is earned. You will learn that lesson over and over again throughout your life. Earning money takes time and effort. As you grow older and you choose to do more around the house, most teens can expect to negotiate a higher allowance. It will be a good training ground for your first job.

Take the time to learn more about how to handle money. Most are willing to keep teens informed on family expenses. You need to know how money is used to pay mortgages, phone bills, insurance, utility payments, food, clothing, medical and dental expenses. There's no need for you to do an extensive audit, but you should see what it takes to keep a family afloat. When you have your own place, you will appreciate understanding the importance of using money wisely. As a slight hint, if this hasn't happened in your home, try showing this paragraph to your parents.

> *"The most patriotic thing I can do for my country is to remain solvent." James E. Sinclair*

Many parents try and give teens choices in managing money. By having to work within a budget for clothes, you will learn the importance of looking at price tags in buying everything. Buying one designer shirt, may cost more than three quality garments without the name label. When you make the choices, you get to live with the benefits and the consequences of those choices. You will have similar choices to make throughout your life. Learning to live by a budget while you are young will help you manage your resources effectively as an adult.

> *"He who will not economize will have to agonize." Confucius*

> *"Beware of little expenses; a small leak will sink a great ship."* Benjamin Franklin

If you decide to get a job, you will learn the importance of overcoming frustration and refusals on your way to your first job. You will learn the importance of references and recommendations. As a result, **be less concerned about the**

94

pay you receive. Be more concerned about the contacts and experiences you can gain. A good work experience can be a credential builder for your future. With most jobs you will learn the importance of appearance, customer service, and a positive attitude. **In short, holding a job can help you learn the "work ethic" that has made many a person successful.** Job holding can promote responsibility, build character, and promote maturity. Take every job seriously--it is part of your employment history.

At the same time, working part-time can override other very important values--having fun as a teenager and getting a good education. Working hard at getting an education is critical for your personal growth and eventual professional success. Enjoying social relationships as a teen is also important in becoming an adult. Balancing these priorities is not always easy in today's crowded teenage schedule. **It is suggested that most parents limit their teen's time at work to no more than 10-15 hours a week.** Most parents want no horror stories of a dazed, bone-weary teenager stumbling through his classes and watching his grades tumble and his social life grind to a halt.

There are many jobs available for teenagers today and the money teenagers have earned has brought them more buying power. But it has also left many teenagers disinterested in school and hooked as materialism junkies buying CD's, designer clothes, and status cars at the expense of learning self-discipline. Some have called the problem "premature affluence"; instead of learning the value of a buck, they have the mistaken idea that money is available to satisfy any passing whim.

There is a valuable middle ground where some work is healthy and too much is a problem for school and an adequate social life. **Work with your parents and your boss to set up a work schedule that will leave time and energy to keep school and having fun as a teen a top priority while still giving you some opportunity to learn the value of work.** Work to find what you can handle.

To help teens learn the value of money, many parents limit the money teens are allowed to spend; some funds will be saved for the future. Some parents will go so far as to require a portion of what you earn be used for general household expenses. It's understandable that when you benefit from living in your home, you may also be expected to contribute to its upkeep. Whether your parents need it or not, you can benefit from learning that most of the money you earn in life goes for necessities, not the luxuries. Earning less money now may be frustrating, but doing well in school, learning how to save, and developing social skills will help prepare you for earning much more later in life. It will also help you develop the maturity to manage your money when you do begin to earn a larger salary.

"I had eight boys and we had one rule about money. Any money they earned in part-time jobs was divided in three ways: 50% they could spend; 25% goes to savings; and 25% goes to the home fund to pay for maid support for mom." Anonymous

"Credit Card Warning: Using this card could be hazardous to your wealth. The interest rates cause vomiting, nausea, and diarrhea." Anonymous

Even if parents had the available wealth, most would be reluctant to give their teen a blank check to buy whatever they wanted with their money. **The real world seldom provides a free ride; few parents will either.** Spoiled people don't learn to rely on themselves. Instead, they keep waiting for the big break--that big lottery in the sky that will give them their millions. Learning to save, work, and budget limited resources is never as glamorous as winning a lottery, but it works. Learning that now will be well worth it when you're on your own. Welcome to the frustration, the challenge, and the satisfaction of making ends meet.

"Capital as such is not evil; it is its wrong use that is evil." Mohandas Gandhi

"What good is it for a man to gain the whole world, yet forfeit his soul? For what shall a man give in exchange for his soul?" Mark 8:36-37

As important as money is, never let money become a god waiting to take your soul or a barometer of your, or any man's self-respect. No matter what you make, save, or do, every person has value. Never forget to treat all people that way.

"My mama used to say to me, 'If you have a piece of bread, break it into three pieces: One for today's sustenance, one for tomorrow's, and the third to give to someone with no bread at all.'" *Al Waxman, Canadian Actor*

"Riches either serve or govern the possessor." *Horace*

15

Study Hard to Find Your Place in the Future

"It's just that you don't want to do it yet. And all it'll take is maybe leaving you out in the wilderness with no food or money in the middle of winter. Just a dime to make a collect call saying that you're ready to study." Bill Cosby

"We are all born ignorant, but one must work hard to remain stupid." Benjamin Franklin

"Ignorance doesn't kill you, but it makes you sweat a lot." Haitian Proverb

"There will always be prayer in the schools...as long as there are final exams." Anonymous

There is a place in the future for everyone. Whether you strive to find your place remains your decision, and it requires your effort. **One of life's big mistakes is to think you're working for someone else.** No matter what you do, you're working for yourself. Too many youth say that their parents or teachers make them do it. If you're not motivated, the person who suffers the most is you. Getting an "F" because you don't like a teacher or a subject doesn't hurt the teacher. It hurts you! Remember, whose "F" is it? You may ask, "What's the big deal? Who's going to care ten years from now?" You may care! **Learn early not to blame the bearer of bad grades; look in the mirror for the**

real culprit. It's time to take hold of your own opportunities and stop blaming others.

> *"Those who don't read books have no advantage over those who can't read them." Mark Twain*

> *"The shortest distance between poverty and wealth is education." Robert C. Allen*

> *"A wise man has great power, and a man of knowledge increases strength." Proverbs 24:5*

Teens often use teachers as an excuse for not learning. We understand that all teachers are not created equal. Most start with high ideals and commitment, but some burn out in overcrowded classrooms with underpaid support. Some choose to remain and coast in rooms with teenagers they are sure would rather be somewhere else. Most are fair. Many are enthusiastic and find a way to flourish even with the limitations. **You will have your share of good and bad teachers, but it remains your responsibility to find a way to work with each teacher you have.** Be thankful for the good ones. Find a way to work with the others.

> *"You can complain all you want outside, but inside this classroom you will apply yourself, and I will never teach down to you. One day, one of you little rascals may run for governor or President, and you will be prepared." Jesse Jackson's teacher, Mrs. Shelton*

> *"Don't work hard only when your master is watching and then shirk when he isn't looking; work hard and with gladness all the time, as though working for Christ, doing the will of God with all your heart." Ephesians 6:6-7*

Alvin Toffler, a noted futurist, has said that, **"The illiterate of the future are not those that cannot read or write, but**

those that cannot learn, unlearn and relearn." Your education won't end with high school or college. You may get to pick the subjects you want to study, but you will still be learning all your life. It has been said that, "Some people forget to update their minds." Don't let that happen to you. The career you select for college is most likely not what you will be doing all your life. Some futurists suggest you will have up to six careers in your life time. Change will be the name of the game.

"The mind is like a muscle, which no good American would admit neglecting--it must be exercised, stretched until it hurts a little, every day. In return it becomes stronger, more flexible and more enjoyable to use." Robert C. Solomon

"Then, why go to school?" you might ask. It is true that many things you learn in school may never be used. That's

not the reason you are in school; **you are learning how to learn--how to apply yourself to learn a new skill and to master it.** That is a self-discipline habit you must have to

101

be successful in the future whatever you do. You don't skip steps on the ladder to success.

"If I went back to college again, I'd concentrate on two areas: learning to write, and to speak before an audience. Nothing in life is more important than the ability to communicate effectively." Gerald R. Ford

Getting great grades in school is not the only goal worth working for. Sure, getting straight "A's" will open many doors that otherwise you would not be able to use. **Getting into a certain college or career requires good grades. If you want such a career, you will need to motivate yourself to get high grades.** But there are many other doors that do not require straight "A's". However, **all worthwhile doors require the ability to learn and the ability to do a job well.**

"If you think education is expensive, try ignorance." Derek Bok

"In 1979 the average male college graduate aged 25 to 34 earned 18% more than a high school graduate of the same age. By 1986 the advantage had jumped to 43%...." Frank S. Levy, University of Maryland

Don't be panicked or discouraged by a bad grade; it's not the end of the world. But do learn to bounce back and apply yourself, or you're just putting off the inevitable. Some day you will have to do something well enough to get paid for it. In our age of plastic credit cards and checks that are deposited and never seen, it's not easy for teens to learn the economic facts of life. All parents have had to learn how to make money to meet their responsibilities and fuel their dreams. In fact, you were probably one of their very special dreams. They had to work hard to be able to afford to have you. It won't be long before you will have the same opportunity to make your dreams happen.

102

"A jet plane burns its greatest energy taking off; but once it reaches its cruising altitude, it burns less fuel. Just like studying. If you're constantly taking off and landing, you're going to burn more fuel as opposed to taking off and staying up there and maintaining the altitude." Bill Cosby

You will never be great at **everything**. You don't have time to, and you don't need to. Learn to specialize in something that you enjoy and that others are willing to pay for. You'll learn to strive for "A's" in the things that matter and, if you must, "C's" in the things that are not as important. **Being a perfectionist in everything is a curse no one would wish on you.** It is important for you to find what you're good at and be able to do a quality job when it counts. That's what school is really about. **School provides a chance to find and cultivate your strengths and to learn how to develop the self-discipline to apply yourself when you need to.**

"The only true measure of success is the ratio between what we might have been on one hand, and the thing we have made ourselves on the other." H.G. Wells

"Education takes many forms. Most forms are through the school system, but other forms of education are just as important. Take the time to listen: You'll be surprised how much knowledge people have to share." Malcolm-Jamal Warner, "Theo" from The Bill Cosby Show

Don't worry about getting an education just to please teachers or parents--finding your place in the world is your adventure that only starts in school. Too many waste valuable years resisting education only to find that later in life they have to make up valuable time by going back to school. **Don't waste your school years, use them.** By using your high school years to apply yourself, you take advantage of a time when you have fewer distractions and your parents are paying your way. When you put off working hard, you may very well have to make up for your lack of high school effort by paying for your own education and taking valuable time you could have had to enjoy the fruits of your early labors. You only go through high school once; take advantage of it. Don't worry! **You can learn and have fun in high school; it's just smart to do both!**

"Not to know is bad; not to wish to know is worse." African Proverb

Just remember the most important message--you are more than your grades! No matter what you end up putting on your business card, or whether you have one for that matter, your parents love you for who you are--their child.

"Thomas Edison was labeled 'too stupid to learn.' Winston Churchill was called 'dull and hopeless' and flunked sixth grade. Walt Disney, who loved to sketch and draw, was told he had no talent. Abraham Lincoln did not allow himself to wallow in these failures: 1832-lost job and was defeated for legislature; 1833-failed in private business; 1836-had nervous breakdown and was defeated for house speaker; 1843-was defeated for nomination to Congress; 1854-defeated for Senate; 1856-defeated for nomination for Vice President; 1858-defeated for Senate again." Catherine Feste

"It is never too late to be what you might have been." George Elliot

16

Say "No" to Drugs and Alcohol

"About the only beneficial thing in smoking is that it repels gnats and mosquitoes. Which only proves you don't have to be big to be smart." Paul Sweeney

"One reason that I don't drink is that I want to know when I'm having a good time." Lady Astor

We have one major message--never become a slave to any habit that will detract from your ability to live a full life. Why do teens use alcohol or drugs? Is it to celebrate? To have fun? To get rid of problems? To get happy? To feel more relaxed with friends? To rebel against their parents? To experiment? To impress dates or to just be cool? Whatever the excuse, there is no such thing as responsible use of an illegal substance. There is no logic in taking or smoking something that is abusing your body. We understand that life can be confusing at times--no life is immune to problems and pressures, but no problem or pressure is worth giving your body over to any drug.

"What is dangerous about the tranquilizers is that whatever peace of mind they bring is a packaged peace of mind. Where you buy a pill and buy peace with it, you get conditioned to cheap solutions instead of deep ones." Max Lerner

You've heard the toxic effects of alcohol and drugs until you're sick of hearing them. But the facts speak for themselves. True, there are many people who drink and still manage not to die young, beat their partners, or drive under the influence. There are millions who drink socially and never become alcoholics. But you never know when the roulette wheel will land on your number. Most adults

take an occasional drink because they enjoy it. Most do not have a drink every day; they do not "need" alcohol.

"Woe unto those that rise early in the morning to run after their drinks, who stay up late at night till they are inflamed with wine." Isaiah 5:11

"If you have ever asked yourself whether you are addicted, you are. You wouldn't be considering it, if you weren't." Anonymous

But why can't teens "enjoy" alcohol like adults seem to do? First, it's against the law. **When you are of legal drinking age, the choice will be yours, as will the responsibility.** You may feel you are ready now and two or three years will make little difference. Most adults could understand your point of view, but collectively, society has found that the historical data is against you. When teens have had the right to drink, many teens have not used alcohol responsibly. The laws you want to rebel against are the unfortunate result. Try and be patient. Your time to drink will come soon enough. If you can avoid its use now, it will be even easier for you to control as an adult.

"Steriods...have been linked to reduced fertility,...increased aggressiveness,...liver damage,...cardiovascular disease, acne,...and cutting short a child's long-term physical development by briefly accelerating, then shutting off, bone growth." Janny Scott

"Crack is the most diabolical form of a harmful substance to make its appearance this century. Because it comes wrapped and coated like Christmas candy.... It is like death wearing a bridal dress, the big rock candy mountain with a volcano inside. It is turning America into a horror movie." Columnist Jim Murray

If you are going to fight off the influence of drugs, you will have to learn to say a few "very" important words. One of the most important words in any language is "NO!" **Be tough enough to say "NO!"**, but you have to mean it. The exact words you choose to say aren't important. Just find your own message you are comfortable with and think it through before you have to say it. **Be assertive but non-judgemental,** "No thanks. If you want to do it, that's up to you, but I'd rather not." "Drugs are boring. I don't need drugs to feel good; I can do it on my own." "Hey, I may have to drive." If they persist, try being more direct, "Stop pushing me! I already told you 'no.' If you were my friend, you would back off on this." If all else fails, try blaming parents, "Look, I promised my folks." It may be hard to say "no" to your peers, but beating the habit once you're on drugs or hooked on alcohol is even harder. If some friends reject you for taking a stand, what kind of friends are they? **True friends respect your right to be you.**

"There comes a time when you have to plant your feet, stand firm, and make a point about who you are." Pat Riley

"A group of friends...decided...it would be more fun to get stoned. As they all started piling in the car, my head was contemplating. I said, 'No thank you; I'm going to school.' As they drove off one way and I walked the other way, the feeling of accomplishment filled my body. With every step I took toward school I felt strong that I was going to do something with my life, that I was going to be somebody. Just take one day at a time and I'll get toward where I want to go." Maribeth All

Understand that the commitment to stand firm has to come from within. Only you can make that decision and show that you mean it. The preacher can preach, the writer can write, the politicians can pass laws, but nothing will happen for you unless you say to yourself, "I choose to say 'no' to drugs in my life." Gain strength in self-discipline by practicing saying "no" to the little choices at school. Let people know you don't use it. As you are successful in small battles, you begin counting on the same weapon--the word "no"--to win the major wars against alcohol and drug abuse that face you at almost every teen party.

Set your own standards and be a positive model for others. By knowing your limits you can provide strength to all those who want to say "no" but don't have the courage to stand alone.

> *"Every time someone does drugs or sells drugs, or even just looks the other way, they are supporting an industry that costs more than money, it costs lives.... Drugs are...an equal opportunity destroyer, they have no conscience. I am asking you not to look the other way. You...know who's got a problem. Today I am not just asking you to get help, I'm asking you to find someone who needs you and offer to help.... If you're not in trouble, help someone who is. You're here to make a difference, for yourself and those around you. So learn to count on each other. Take care of each other. Give someone else another chance...."* George Bush

If your faith is important to you, ask God for the strength to stand firm. **God calls our bodies the temple of God, so don't mess up the furnishings by bringing in drugs.** What you cannot do for yourself, God can help do for you if you lean on Him during the tough temptations. Prayer can give you strength any time you call on its power. Do it frequently.

There is also nothing wrong with seeking professional help if you need it. You can gain added strength, guidance, and support through caring people who are trained to help.

As for smoking, it is a waste of one's health, as well as one's money. A pack a day will cost you close to $1,000 a year. Can you think of things you would rather spend money on? We're sure you can.

> *"The number of minutes you spend puffing on cigarettes is the number of minutes you shorten your lives by smoking. It is as if you are making a pact with the devil. You are trading a minute off your life for every minute you 'enjoy' a cigarette. This may amount to a decade of life for a serious smoker."* Pamela Canter

If you are already smoking, take a look in the mirror the next time you light up. Ask yourself the questions: "Why am I doing this?" "Is it worth it?" If and when you choose to give up the habit, do not expect it to be easy. But it is achievable with persistent effort to keep "stopping" until you stop. If you need to say "no" to peer pressure, try one of these messages on for size: "No thank you--allergies." "No thanks. I'm in sports, and if the coach doesn't kill me for smoking, the wind sprints will." Finally, if you should choose to smoke anyway, do not smoke in your house or with people you in any way care about. Passive smoke is not a gift anyone wants to receive, nor is it one you want to give.

"Try exhaling three breathes in succession without inhaling. What you have left is what you live on when you have emphysema. When I heard that and tried it, I stopped smoking that day." Dottie Moore

Don't forget your parents. When you most feel like moving away from them, you can use their support. Try asking for their help, and you may be pleasantly surprised by how positively they respond. Remember one final thing, **you can have a good time without drugs, without alcohol and without smoking.** It can be done.

"It may seem to you that your parents and your teachers grew up in simpler times. But most of them lived through the civil rights struggles. Some of your fathers fought in Vietnam. And for many of you, your parents and teachers were among the first to face drugs. If you care enough to talk to them, you might be surprised at how much they do understand...." George Bush

Nat. Clearing House for Alcohol and Drug Inf.: 301-468-2600
National Institute of Drug Abuse Hotline: 1-800-662-4357
Parents Resource Inst. for Drug Ed. (PRIDE): 1-800-677-7433
STRAIGHT: 1-800-937-4363

17

Don't Drink and Drive or Get into a Car with Someone Who Has Been Drinking

"Before I'll drive with a drunk, I'll drive myself." Stevie Wonder

"Drive drunk and you could have a date with death. Get caught, and all your dates will be with mom." Anonymous

"If the thought of losing your life doesn't keep you from drinking and driving, imagine losing your license." Anonymous

"In the annals of parent brutality (which include summer school attendance, forced feeding of fresh broccoli and speaking to their kids in public), nothing is considered more inhumane to teenagers than taking away their cars." Erma Bombeck

The lecture is simple--Don't drive drunk or ride with anyone who has been drinking. Your life is not the only one that could be lost. Too many teens and adults who "feel they can handle their alcohol" have been "dead" wrong. Their impaired driving has resulted in innocent people dying in an unnecessary and tragic accident. Even if the drunk driver survives, he is left to cope with a living hell knowing he cost the life of another. You have too much to live for to risk letting that happen. Drive sober as a teen

111

and as an adult. **As long as you are a true friend to your buddies, you won't let them drive under the influence either.** True friends care enough to take a stand against driving and alcohol.

"In 1987, highway accidents killed 3,259 youths 15 to 19. Half were blamed on alcohol." National Commission Against Drunk Driving

"Don't drink and drive. We have not another loved one to spare." The inscription on the Radcliff, Kentucky memorial to the 27 who where killed by a drunk driver in their infamous 1988 bus crash

Every parent knows that uncomfortable feeling of seeing their teen drive off for an evening of fun with the "gang." No parent wants anything to happen to their children, and, unfortunately, they know they have no control over the competency or the sobriety of any of your chauffeurs. So please understand how strongly parents feel. **They won't care about the time or the cost of the call, just call if there is a problem.** They will pay for the collect call, and most will pay for a taxi if you feel your drive home might not be safe. We know how tough it is to be comfortable calling, but trust them. No matter how inconvenienced or disappointed they might be at the moment, your parents wouldn't want you to risk your life or the life of others by getting into a car with an unreliable driver or attempting yourself to drive under the influence of alcohol. **A call or taxi bill, no matter what the time or the amount, is a small price to pay for your safety.**

We don't want you to drink; you know how we feel about drugs and alcohol. But if you or your friends do drink, do it responsibly. **Take the time to pick your designated driver, and then make sure that he doesn't drink.** Volunteering to take the role yourself will give you a way to handle the peer pressure to use alcohol. You can get used to saying, "Not me. I'm the designated 'sober' here!"

If you really care about your friends that are driving, you will learn how to look out for them. Practice some messages you are comfortable saying that will still get the message across: "I'd sleep a lot better if I knew you wouldn't be driving home tonight;" "Here's a soda on me;" "You might try eating something between drinks. By now, the alcohol has drowned everything in there." Get your friends drinking soft drinks, eating solid foods, and away from more alcohol. Nothing truly sobers up a drunk quickly, so insist on driving them home instead of letting them drive. Too many teens and adults often misjudge their ability to handle driving when they have been drinking even small amounts of alcohol.

"I don't want to ride with you this way! I don't care how far it is. I'd rather walk! At least I'll get there." Anonymous

"Silence gives consent." Thomas Fuller

"To be modest in speaking truth is hypocrisy." Kahlil Gibran

"The smaller the drink, the clearer the head." William Penn

Now for the consequences of not using good judgement. **If you ever give your parents any reason to believe that you have driven their car, your own, or anyone else's car while intoxicated, expect consequences.** In most states, parents can have the license of a minor suspended for one year. In extreme cases many parents will not hesitate to use such measures. Most will not give you the tests the police would provide, intoxicated behavior will usually be enough. They're not detectives. They won't have to know what you did or didn't drink. They will go by what they see. Justice in the home isn't perfect, but it only takes one time to kill or maim yourself or others. Don't test your parents; call them for their help before you risk being caught.

"If they are drinking in your car, you get the ticket." Anonymous

What parents expect from you, they should do as well. Discuss this topic with your parents and ask them to promise to control their use of alcohol as well. Most parents will agree to limit their consumption of alcohol before driving and to refuse a ride with other adults that don't. Your parents shouldn't expect you to act responsibly, if they do not act that way themselves. Being a parent and worrying about your behavior, should make them aware of how you might worry about them as well.

This lecture for all of us can be summed up in three sentences. **If you are driving tonight, don't drink. If you are drinking, please don't drive. Finally, don't ride with any driver who has been drinking.** Now that we understand the limits, let's all choose to live by them daily.

DRINKING AND DRIVING CONTRACT

I agree to call you for advice and/or transportation at any hour, from any place if I am ever in a situation where I have had too much to drink or a friend or date who is driving me has had too much to drink or is acting in a way that indicates it may not be safe to ride with them.

Teen Signature_____Date_____

I agree to come to get you at any hour, any place, or I will pay for a taxi to bring you safely home. I will do this in a positive manner, asking no questions and starting no argument at that time. I would also expect to discuss this incident at a later time.

I also agree to seek safe and sober transportation home if I have had too much to drink or a friend who is driving me has had too much to drink or is acting in a manner that would suggest that I seek another form of transportation.

Parent Signatures_____Date_____

This contract is adapted from the "Contract For Life" developed by SADD (Students Against Drunk Driving). For copies of their contract or information on starting a group in your area, contact SADD, P.O. Box 800, Marlboro, MA 01752 or call (508)481-3568.

18

Take Care of Your Body

"Fat doesn't like to get used; it likes to be stored. I graduated from high school 'Magna Cum Lardo!'" Candy Cummings, R.D.

"I know I need exercise, but would you mind running for me?" Anonymous

"Pamper yourself. There is no replacement." All the lectures aside, that says it all. God has given us one body and asks us to be wise stewards in our journey through life. "Be careful!" "Eat right!" "Get out of that chair and get some exercise!" Those are messages you get tired of hearing, but they hit a chord even adults sometimes resist hearing-- **"Take care of your body, or it may not take care of you!"**

"He that takes medicine and neglects to diet wastes the skill of his doctors." Chinese Proverb

"Run in such a way that you may win. Everyone who competes in the games exercises self-control in all things." 1 Corinthians 9:24-25

This isn't a call to run 50 miles a week. It isn't a crusade to banish all french fries and hot fudge sundae's. Being "fit" is being "healthy" and that doesn't mean having a body like a superstar athlete or a fashion model. **This is a call for balance in a hope of building positive exercise and eating habits that will give you a safe and sensible lifestyle you**

can live with for the long haul. It's having a body that's ready to go. You can run a couple of miles or spend an evening dancing without having to have an ambulance ready.

"The key to cardiovascular fitness is consistency rather than intensity." Dr. James Rippe

"Fear less, hope more; eat less, chew more; whine less, breathe more; talk less, say more; hate less, love more; and all good things are yours." Swedish Proverb

There was a funny, but dangerous, dessert bar sign that read, "Life is uncertain; eat dessert first." There's some truth in that admonition, but don't take it to extremes. **Let yourself go out to have a sundae, on occasion, but don't invite such temptations into your home.** Even the most disciplined will give in to an Oreo cookie when it's in the same room. Learn to love healthy foods by trying to cultivate a taste for whole grains, fruits, vegetables, and low fat meat and dairy products. **Sugar isn't the big enemy-- fats are!** Limit the cheeseburgers, fried foods, butter, cheese, and ice cream. But limiting does not mean eliminating everything; just make fatty foods the exception, not the norm.

"The first wealth is health." Ralph Waldo Emerson

"Countless people tell me they would like to eat better, but they don't want to 'give up' tasty food. Rather than thinking about what they can't have, they should think about what they can eat." Sybil Stanton

What about exercise? Mark Twain once said, "When it comes to exercise, engage in both sleeping and resting. I never could see a benefit in being tired." Many seem to agree. Too many parents and teens become couch potatoes, sitting around watching instead of doing. It's a mistake to "leave the running to the jocks!" Being cool may leave you "terminal cool" at fifty. Besides, Mark Twain was wrong. **Research supports that regular exercise results in a higher energy level. Teens that are out of shape are the ones that tire quickest.**

You don't have to overdose on exercise to get a benefit; go for something you can enjoy and live with. Going on an "all or nothing" diet and exercise crusade, is one of the best ways to insure that you will soon relapse into old habits. Look for small changes to increase your health habit batting average every day; bounce back from the bad days to do better tomorrow. Associate with friends that support exercise and healthy eating habits. Don't just watch sports; participate. When possible, instead of driving, ride your bike or walk. When you and your friends go to the mall, walk briskly when you talk. Work up and maintain a good sweat three to four times a week for at least 20 minutes. Anything more than that, do because you love it or you want to lose extra weight. If you like to eat, learn to like to exercise. People who regularly exercise burn more calories even when they are not exercising than people who don't make exercise a part of their routine.

> "We are under-exercised as a nation. We look instead of play. We ride instead of walk. Our existence deprives us of the minimum of physical activity essential for healthy living." John F. Kennedy

> "Lack of activity destroys the good condition of every human being, while movement and methodical physical exercise saves it and preserves it." Plato

> "A vigorous five mile walk will do more good for an unhappy but otherwise healthy adult than all the medicine and psychology in the world." Dr. Paul Dudley White

Life is too precious to waste because of poor health habits. Even small adjustments to the rudder of a ship leads to major changes in where the ship ends up. Making small changes now in your eating and exercise habits will do the same for your health now, as well as later in life. Take care of your body, and it will take care of you. **Learning good habits now will let you enjoy them for life.**

> "Do you not know that your body is a temple of the Holy Spirit, who is in you, whom you have received from God? You are not your own; you were bought at a price. Therefore honor God with your body." I Corinthians 6:19,20

19

Let Me Know Where You Are, So We Won't Worry

"Half of life is showing up." Woody Allen

"What do you mean you forgot to call? I'm going to forget to let you out of your room. Do you want me to forget that?" Anonymous

It's probably as difficult for your parents as it is for you to go through your transition into adult independence. When you were a child, they were used to protecting you, watching after your every move, making sure you found your way--all those things parents should do for "little kids" in a world that can be unforgiving for children who are not cautious. Your parents understand that you are no longer so little, but it takes time for their feelings and their habits to catch up with your growing older. When you work with them to help them let go, it works smoother. When you fight them, they tend to hold on tighter.

When it comes to worrying, parents usually major in it. It may seem unnecessary to you; "no problem," right? Give your parents a break. They've made it through this far, and they want to make sure you make it the rest of the way. **Humor them by giving them the information that they need to feel you're safe. They care.** What you see is their frustration, but what you can't see are their feelings. They know that they have to let go, they even want to. But it's not easy.

Your freedoms will come quicker when your parents trust your judgement and you meet their need for assurance that your decisions are mature. You can give evidence of that by keeping them informed on where you're going--a simple note, a two minute call, a message on their answering machine--it doesn't take much. Most parents understand that sometimes they're not that easy to check in with; they live busy lives as well. But that makes it even more

important to communicate your plans early. Over time, as they develop more trust, you will be able to do less checking and more reporting.

in hiding of the fault than did the fault before it was so patched."
Shakespeare

"There is no waste of time in life like that of making explanations."
Benjamin Disraeli

"They say things, and do not do them." Matthew 23:3

Keep enough change to call; take the time to use it. Don't let money be the issue; they'll reimburse you for any money you use. We realize that some parents will not have their teens report in. Maybe they have established an adequate trust; maybe they never needed to. **Every parent and teen must take their own path and earn their own trust.** Help your parents make your path smooth by taking the time to let them know where you are. After a while, they will get bored of it, and, by then, you will be used to the habit. At that point, you will be well on your way to establishing the common courtesy that people who care let the people they love know where they are and where they will be. **Family members worry when loved ones aren't where they should be, not because they don't trust, but because they care.** Your parents care about you; help them do that without having to repeat this frustrating lecture.

"All idle reasons lessen the weight of the good ones you gave before." Jonathan Swift

"What must be revealed eventually should be revealed immediately." Anonymous

122

20

Be Careful When You Drive

"My dad didn't actually refuse to buy me a car. He just thought I ought to become more familiar with running simpler machines. He's letting me start on the lawn mower." Anonymous

"The only midnight oil my son knows how to burn is gasoline." Anonymous

"Won't you give me any money to buy a car? Sure, I'll match what your friends will give you." Anonymous

"A young man was told if he wanted a car he had to 'get good grades, save some money, and cut your hair.' After doing the first two, he asked if he could forget the last requirement arguing that 'Jesus Christ had long hair.' His father replied, 'That makes my point. You've never heard of Jesus Christ driving a car either.'" Anonymous

If you're like most teenagers, after the age of sixteen, you begin to plot, prepare, and beg for a driver's license and a car. Parents think you all must have learned it in a seminar on "How To Be A Teenager." But most parents can understand. A license and access to a car means status to your peers. It means independence and freedom to go where you want to go. In one sentence; it means adulthood is on the way.

"On his 14th birthday, a teen-ager will start the countdown on his march to a driver's license. 'Only 730 more days...17,520

hours...426 more days of conning Mom into driving me to school...two more crummy vacations in the back seat, and then...the car is mine. I'm history!'" Erma Bombeck

In many ways your parents look forward to your driving. There will be less chauffeuring. For a while at least, you will love to do errands--anything to drive a car. It will also be nice to have you share in the driving on long trips. So guess what? It's not just you that wants you to be able to drive. Most parents want you to be able to get behind the wheel, too.

Most parents want you to be able to drive, but they want you to drive safely and responsibly. They want no "road warriors" racing through their community. That's why most insist that you take the high school driver's education and training course. They will help teach you the rules, provide driving experience, and when completed may reduce your insurance costs. Trained instructors will probably do a better job than your parents could in teaching you. Paid driving instructors train teens all the time and are probably more relaxed in the role.

"Hitting the dashboard at 35 mph is like falling off a three-story building head first. Wear a seatbelt." Anonymous

"If you're not wearing a seatbelt, what's holding you back?" Anonymous

"The price of a mistake shouldn't be a death sentence." Anonymous

Most families are fairly typical when it comes to basic driving ground rules. When you drive the car, you pay for the gas and wash the car. You will pay for all your own parking tickets. In addition to paying for moving violations, your driving privileges may be suspended for serious offenses. Finally, **make sure all in the car have their seat belts on before your foot hits the pedal.**

Remember, "going along with the crowd" may be fine in some areas, but not wise if the "crowd" is breaking any driving laws. **Driving a vehicle can be scary at any speed. When it is not done responsibly, it can be a deadly weapon.** If your parents see you or hear reports of you driving unsafely, they will most likely limit or revoke your driving privileges for a period of time. Since you understand that, the decision remains yours.

> *"There's a way to help teens survive to become good drivers. It's simple. Have a bumper sticker that reads, 'If I'm driving irresponsibly, call my parents.' Then use a black marker to write the parents' phone number. Just knowing that you're driving around with your phone number visible to everybody will be an incentive to drive more responsibly." Fred Stengle*

Even if you drive safely, learn the value of defensive driving and stay attentive. Act like you're driving in a swarm of lunatics. In many areas, that might very well be accurate! Being prepared for the unexpected means keeping your eyes focused well down the road to anticipate traffic problems. Give ample distance between cars and be aware of moves you can make if problems occur. Giving room and maintaining attentive visibility are the defensive driver's greatest assets. Safe driving means keeping your eyes off of your stereo buttons and your other passengers and on the job of driving. Safe driving means keeping your car interior clear of trash that may obstruct easy access to your foot pedals.

"Driving is merely a repetition of three basic actions. See-Think-Do. Another way of saying this is, perceive-predict-perform. You must see trouble. You must predict what action is necessary. You must perform such action-in time." The Smith System

"The Five Keys to Space System Driving: Aim high in steering; get the big picture; keep your eyes moving; leave yourself an out; and make sure they see you." The Smith System

"You are ready for defensive driving. There are six things you can do to ensure a safe journey:
*Scan Ahead. (Be ready to) reduce speed, turn on lights and ascertain where you stand in the traffic flow.
*Check Behind. (Be ready to take) evasive action.
*Keep Your Distance. (leave space to avoid) abrupt stops or lane changes in heavy traffic.
*Be Alert To Head-Ons. If confronted by an oncoming vehicle, your best bet is to reduce speed and move as far as possible to the right. If you must hit, turn your car at an angle.
*Take Care At Intersections. Approach with your foot off the accelerator and over the brake pedal; look left, then right, then left again before proceeding.
*Practice Patience and Courtesy. The essence of defensive driving is the art of anticipating and avoiding hazards." Stanley L. Englebardt, "Drive Defensively--and Live"

Don't forget to compute the condition of your car in the safe driving equation. **You are only as good a driver as the vehicle you use allows you to be.** Check your tires, brakes, oil, and other vital systems. "But it costs money!" you plead. Yes, it does, but preventive maintenance saves you money in the long run. A well known oil filter ad has a mechanic holding an inexpensive filter as he says, **"Pay me now or pay me later".** The ad's focus turns to an auto up in the air having its engine replaced. So much of life is learning to take good care of things so they last. A car will teach you that lesson quickly. Don't take a "drive it until you trash it" approach. The cost is more than the car; it could be your life or the lives of others.

Welcome to the joy and the responsibilities of driving. You'll like it, and it certainly does beat walking! By the way, if you clean your parents' car more frequently, they may even let you use it.

"You wouldn't have any trouble in school if you put the same enthusiasm for getting ahead as you show on the freeways!" *Anonymous*

"Drive carefully--your car is not the only thing that can be recalled by its maker." *Anonymous*

21

Take Time to Know Your God

"Whenever I go past a church I always stop and visit. I want to make sure that when they carry me in, the Lord won't ask, 'Who is it?'" Anonymous

"An atheist is a man with no visible means of support." John Buchan, Lord Tweedmuir

"In this life you sometimes have to choose between pleasing God and pleasing man. In the long run it's better to please God--he's more apt to remember." Harry Kemelman

Your way doesn't have to be your parents' way, but find a way to keep God your partner in your walk through life. In effect, make a merger with God, and his power will be with you. Practice depending upon him and praying to him for support and strength.

"God is like a mirror. The mirror never changes but everybody who looks at it sees something different." Rabbi Harold Kushner

You will find that your teenage years will cause you to question your faith. You will question many things in these turbulent years; that questioning is necessary. You may want tangible proof. Unfortunately, it is unlikely that God will come to you in physical form and talk you into believing in him. Many see his handiwork in the beauty of nature, but don't be limited to such proof.

Study scripture for yourself and look at the lives of believers you respect. Does their faith make a difference in their lives? Do you want to have some of the qualities they possess? If your answer is "Yes", invest the time in coming close to God, even if it is not always popular with your peers.

> *"There was a culture shock in coming back (from Ethiopia). I didn't feel like I had left a desert. I felt like I was coming home to one. What I saw was that we have so much in the West, but so little. Though we physically are so fat, we are spiritually starving to death." U2's Bono Hewson*

> *"Without the assistance of that Divine Being..., I cannot succeed. With that assistance, I cannot fail. Trusting in Him who can go with me, and remain with you, and be everywhere for good, let us confidently hope that all will yet be well." Abraham Lincoln*

God will not require all of your time. He won't stop you from enjoying your teen years. **He's not here to punish you. He's here to bring you joy and peace!**

129

"Have you not heard? The Lord is the everlasting God, the Creator of the ends of the earth. He will not grow weary, and his understanding no one can fathom. He gives strength to the weary and increases the power of the weak. Even youths grow tired and weary, and young men stumble and fall, but those who hope in the Lord will renew their strength. They will soar on wings of eagles; they will run and not grow weary; they will walk and not be faint." Isaiah 40:28-31

"'Love the Lord your God with all your heart, soul, and mind.' This is the first and greatest commandment. The second most important is similar: 'Love your neighbor as much as you love yourself.'" Matthew 22:37-39

Many parents will ask you to worship with them at their place of worship. If you find a different church or temple that lets you have fun in your faith **and** explore what God has to say to you as a teenager, many parents will let you pick your own place of worship. **Whatever group you choose, be active and have the courage to ask whatever questions you have.** God can handle your honesty even when some people can't. You will find that your faith and your youth group can be an anchor to keep your boat steady through the sometimes topsy-turvy teen years.

"To help us keep the faith, God built into each of us something called a censor. Your censor is persistently powerful, always awake, and invariably factual.... Your censor is not a killjoy. It is a builder of joy! It is for you, not against you. It is your friend. And if you listen to its friendly counsel, and accept it as wise advice that it is, and follow it always, you will have the best in life and be successful as a person." Norman Vincent Peale

"If I could say only one thing to do to counter the badness that hostility brings, I'd say to really practice one of the world's religions. The core philosophy would make it hard to stay hostile. And the practices--the meditation and prayer--would accomplish the relaxation that is so healthy. And the membership and par-

130

ticipation would help you trust other people; you'd have special support." Dr. Redford Williams

Learn to read scripture for guidance. Keep your Bible near you as a ready inspiration. Never use it as a club to attack others or as a crutch to hide from your own responsibilities.

"A thorough knowledge of the Bible is worth more than a college education." President Theodore Roosevelt

"There are only two words repeated 365 times together in the Bible--'Fear not.'" Dr. Mark Victor Hansen

It's easy to come to God when you need His help; we all do that. But keep Him with you in the victories as well. You all know "pits people." They love to complain--"School's the pits! Teacher's are the pits! Parents are the pits! You're the pits!" Their negativity is contagious. Few of us take the time to think of the gifts we have been given. Even fewer think of giving thanks to God for every victory. **Nothing will start your day off better than thanking God for another day.** Life shouldn't be something we "have to do!" Life is a gift we "get to experience." Keep God with you through the good and the bad of life.

"To be a Christian without prayer is no more possible than to be alive without breathing." Martin Luther

"God's sanctuary is anywhere you and I stop long enough to meet him." Leslie Parrott

Many parents believe that one of the best gifts they can give you is an appreciation for the value of a genuine faith in God. God cares about you personally. He values us all more than any worldly treasure or sacrifice. He understands our fears and our anxieties and reaches out to each of us with love. In a world that tends to pass by in the fast lane of life without even a glance, God has staying power and the promise of meaning and salvation. **Don't leave God out; He has too much to offer!**

"Act as if everything depends on you. And pray as if everything depends on God." Oprah Winfrey's Father

"Draw near to God, and He will draw near to you." James 4:8

22

Do Your Part for Your Country and Vote When You Have the Right

"You know, you're not supposed to fold, spindle, or mutilate this federal form. Washington doesn't like it." "Washington does a few things I don't like too." Anonymous

"We ought to lower the voting age to fourteen. That's when they know everything." Anonymous

From the first grade through high school, most teens have repeated the pledge of allegiance every morning in school. You know the words, but you have had few opportunities to bring those stirring words to life. Unfortunately, it will probably be years before you come to appreciate the privilege we have to live in this great country of ours. This is not to say that our own country does not have its own faults; they are often plainly visible for the world to see. **But our citizens have the right and the privilege to live in a free country where we choose our own leadership and everyone's vote counts.** That is a privilege that was earned by the blood of many men and women in past generations. Don't take that sacrifice lightly by failing to exercise your right and responsibility to vote. That goes beyond finding your local polling place. It requires your time to study the candidates and the issues before voting.

"America is a symphony, not a melting pot.... In a melting pot, the ingredients soon lose their identity. In a symphony, each instrument is an integral part of the whole, adding its unique contribution to the movement yet, never losing its individuality, its tone, or its beauty." William Arthur Ward

"Ask not what your country can do for you, but what you can do for your country." John F. Kennedy

"The ignorance of one voter in a democracy impairs the security of all." John F. Kennedy

Some teens have asked, "Why do we study history?" If you thought it was to get a good grade in high school history class, try looking a little deeper. **Learning about our history allows us to develop an ability to make sound judgements and keep our perspective in these challenging times.** Whether you exercise it or not, most in our country are born into the right of citizenship. Immigrants coming to our country have to earn that right. But for our democracy to thrive it will depend upon citizens who can exercise informed judgement. When you study history, you learn the tragic, the comic, the heroic, and the profound forces that have combined to make our country. You come to understand how hard it is to preserve our heritage while still moving forward to make our country even better. If past generations have managed to do it, so can we. Not only **can** we rise to the occasion; we **must**.

"The old ideas are new again because they're not old, they are timeless: duty, sacrifice, commitment, and a patriotism that finds its expression in taking part and pitching in." George Bush

"Most questions worth asking have no final answers, and no themes worth examining have endings, happy or otherwise. In sum,...the adventure of democracy, the struggle for liberty, equality, and human dignity, is a way of living, not a settled destination." Paul Gagnon

Does one vote matter? Votes have been won and lost by small margins. A President that wins by a margin of three percent has a landslide on his hands. **You never know what race will require your vote. We suggest you vote in all elections you know something about and not at all when you are not prepared. When you prepare and think about your choices, vote.** When you just fill in the blanks on the basis of pretty faces or billboard propaganda, leave the election to people who have studied the issues. Beyond the meaning of any one election, your right to vote should make a difference to every American that has inherited their birthright.

"The true test of civilization is not the census, nor size of cities, nor the crops, but the kind of man that the country turns out." Ralph Waldo Emerson

"There can be no daily democracy without daily citizenship." Ralph Nader

"It's a great country, but you can't live here for free." Will Rogers

"Our privileges can be no greater than our obligations. The protection of our rights can endure no longer than the performance of our responsibilities." John F. Kennedy

You might ask, "What about all the negative campaigning and the corruption in politics?" The only places that perfect people exist are in educational movies and political commercials. Sure, candidates often play propaganda games to become elected, but under today's media microscope, it's hard to hide if you don't have integrity. **Don't let the imperfections of the system and its people stop you from making it the best you can. Get involved!** It's comforting to know we usually have choices between two or more people who want to serve and who have been tested by the press and the public. We get to make those choices for good or bad. It is your country; treat your voting choices with the respect that privilege deserves.

"Never doubt that a small group of thoughtful, committed citizens can change the world. Indeed, it's the only thing that ever has." Margaret Mead

"Few are willing to brave the disapproval of their fellows, the censure of their colleagues, the wrath of their society. Moral courage is a rarer commodity than bravery in battle or great intelligence. Yet it is the one essential, vital quality for those who seek to change a world that yields most painfully to change. And I believe that in this generation those with courage to enter the moral conflict will find themselves with companions from every corner of the globe." Robert Kennedy

We are given the right as a citizen to say what we think, but most don't use that right. **Write letters to your leaders when you're mad; write letters when you're pleased with what they've done.** Learn to be a supporter and a critic. No matter what your opinion of others and their cause, stand up for their right to say it, or you may someday have others try and take that right from you. It will seem crazy some days, but it's worked for over 200 years. With your help, it will work for another 200 and beyond.

136

"I disapprove of what you say, but I will defend to the death your right to say it." Voltaire

"For rulers are not a cause of fear for good behavior, but for evil. Do you want to have no fear of authority? Do what is good, and you will have praise from the same. Render to all what is due them: tax to whom tax is due; custom to whom custom is due; fear to whom fear is due; honor to whom honor is due." Romans 13: 3&7

"Liberty is the only thing you cannot have unless you are willing to give it to others." William Allen White

People in countries all over the world are claiming the freedoms we so easily take for granted. They march in the streets waving banners; they celebrate their new found freedoms with tears and cheers of joy. **As people across the globe struggle for world peace and democratic principles, be ready to do your part to sustain our own country's proud heritage.** It can be expressed simply. Don't take your country and your freedom for granted. **Exercise** your rights **and** your responsibilities as a citizen on a daily basis.

"People who develop the habit of thinking of themselves as world citizens are fulfilling the first requirement of sanity in our time.... More and more, the choice for the world's people is between becoming world warriors or world citizens." Norman Cousins

"At the bottom of all the tributes paid to democracy is the little man, walking into the little booth, with a little pencil, making a little cross on a little bit of paper--no amount of rhetoric or voluminous discussion can possibly diminish the overwhelming importance of that point." Winston Churchill

23

Do Your Part for Mother Nature

"The whites too shall pass....sooner than other tribes. Continue to contaminate your bed and you will one night suffocate in your own waste." Letter from Chief Seattle to President Franklin Pierce, 1855

"If we wear out our earth, where are we going to live." Dr. Layne Longfellow

Earth will survive us. It's a growing question as to whether man will be along for the ride. It took God to create an environment that would support human life. We seem to be working at record speed to destroy his handiwork. Man used to have to adapt to the environment to survive. Now nature is having to adapt to our wasteful habits and we may not like the results. The earth's ozone layer is decreasing, our air and water resources are becoming more and more polluted. We are wasting resources, and you are living in the country that is responsible for much of that waste. It has to change. We are faced daily with growing evidence that if we don't do something to carefully manage the earth's fragile environment, we may very well be sealing the fate of future generations.

"We travel together, passengers in a little space ship, dependent on its vulnerable resources of air and soil; all committed for our safety

138

to its security and peace; preserved from annihilation only by the care, the work, and, I will say, the love we give our fragile craft."
Adlai Stevenson

"We are all passengers together on a boat that we have damaged--not with the cataclysm of war, but with the slow neglect of a vessel we thought was impervious to our abuse. ... Nature was once the great enemy of Man. ... Now we find the we must protect her from ourselves. A better America is a cleaner America." George Bush

"One generation goes, another generation comes, but the earth abides forever." Ecclesiastes 1:4

Can we really do something? **There is never nothing we can do.** It starts with our taking pride in the beauty of our world and doing our part to preserve it.

Every year in the United States each person generates over one ton of waste. We seem to like disposable diapers, lighters, plates, containers, cameras, disposable everything! But when we are finished with what we buy, we don't seem to be too concerned about where we dispose of our possessions. We had all better begin to care.

"It may be that the greatest tragedy of this period of social transition is not the glaring noisiness of the so-called bad people, but the appalling silence of the so-called good people." Martin Luther King

"We need to move beyond the psychology of winning to the psychology of contributing." Dr. Layne Longfellow

We can go beyond not littering; we can pick up for others that don't seem to care. Instead of just throwing things in the trash, we can recycle cans, papers, and reusable waste. If they don't have a recycling center in your community, your family can work with other teens and adults to get one started. We can all buy cars that use unleaded gas and keep them in good running order to minimize our contribution to smog. When we recharge our auto air-conditioning, we can check for leaks and go to a service center that recycles the freon instead of releasing it into the atmosphere. When you save money by changing your own auto oil, invest a little extra time to save the environment by taking the used oil to a recycling center or arrange for a controlled disposal of the oil. When we can, we can all use public transportation, ride a bike, walk, or drive as a group. We can reuse grocery bags and ask for paper, not plastic. Use a mug or a glass, not paper or styrofoam cups; rags, not paper towels. When we can, we can buy food that is packaged in cardboard, not plastic. We can avoid using products that affect the ozone layer. All families can turn down our water heater and take shorter showers to conserve our water and energy resources. While thinking of our bathroom, we can install low-flow faucet aerators and shower heads and put a plastic bottle in our toilet tank.

Even turning off the water while brushing your teeth saves water that quickly adds up if everyone does it. As you can see, there is much we **can** do!

"All it takes for evil to prevail is for enough good people to do nothing." Anonymous

We all need to consume less. The bumper sticker that reads, "He who dies with the most toys wins," is no longer amusing. It is that kind of attitude that is causing many of our environmental problems. We are all going to be declared losers in this insane consumption derby that rewards style and possessions over substance and service. Instead of automatically buying a new item, we can try repairing what we have until it wears out. We can buy and use rechargeable batteries when we can. **We all need to be responsible consumers so we may once again learn to live in harmony with the land that sustains us.**

"The long fight to save wild beauty represents democracy at its best. It requires citizens to practice the hardest of virtues--self-restraint." Edwin Way Teale

Even if we love the way they look, we should avoid buying endangered plants, animals, or products made from exploited animals. Let's try keeping the furs, ivory, skins, and shells on the animals where they belong. We can do our part to save the birds and marine life that fall victim to the ocean hazard of six-pack plastic holder rings by snipping each circle with scissors before we throw them in the garbage.

"What is man without the beasts? If all the beasts were gone, men would die from a great loneliness of the spirit. For whatever happens to the beasts soon happens to man." Chief Seattle, 1854

We can add to the greening of the planet by planting a tree at least once a year. We can buy living Christmas trees and plant them so they can keep on living, doing their job to stop soil erosion and absorb pollutants. We can push for more open space and parks in our community. Work to preserve the natural beauty of national and state parks, and wild riverbank, ocean, or lake preserves. Man's progress through development is seldom an improvement over mother nature.

> *"Find a dirty hillside, creek, canyon, beach, or roadside (You won't have to look far.) Tell the landowner you're going to clean it up. Call newspapers, TV, radio, and tell them what you're doing. Call the city refuse collection department. Ask how to recycle the various types of waste you expect to collect...." The Ecotactics Activist's Checklist*

As one man put it, we need to stop "living as though we have another earth in the trunk." Every day each of us needs to do something to leave our world better for having been in it. We all need to feel that responsibility personally, act locally in our school and our community, and think globally. We are all in this world together. **We can't expect others to do their part until we do ours.**

> *"God said, Let us make man in our image, after our likeness; and let them have dominion over the fish of the sea, and over the fowl of the air, and over the cattle, and over all the earth....God blessed them, and God said unto them, Be fruitful, and multiply, and replenish the earth,...." Genesis 1:26,28*

> *"Our ideals, laws and customs should be based on the proposition that each generation in turn becomes the custodian rather than the absolute owner of our resources--and each generation has the obligation to pass this inheritance on to the future." Alden Whitman*

FINISH HERE!

THE LECTURE TEST

On the answer sheet provided, check the number of **every lecture** message you have heard (or given) in your home in one form or another (The *content* of the message is what is important, not the *exact wording*)

1. Don't be a slob! Put things where they belong.
2. Don't put things off! When you finish it early, you don't have to cram.
3. Don't take yourself so seriously. A sense of humor is one of the best assets you can have.
4. Say "No" to drugs, cigarettes, and alcohol. Never be a slave to any chemical.
5. Don't drink and drive or get into a car with someone who has.
6. Live the Golden Rule--treat others as you want to be treated.
7. Do the best you can. Anything worth doing is worth doing right.
8. Be nice to your enemies. You have to learn to get along with people, even those you don't like.
9. Don't talk back to your parents. Be able to speak up and express your opinions, but show respect to parents, teachers and elders.
10. Take care of your body. Eat a healthy diet, get your exercise and sleep, and work at staying healthy.
11. Speak the truth so that others can trust your words.
12. Take time to practice. Anything worth learning takes practice.

13. Don't give up without trying. You miss every opportunity you never take.

14. Save sex for marriage. It's a mistake to experiment with sex before you are committed.

15. If you choose to have sex, don't have sex without taking precautions.

16. Learn to save your money, or you won't have money when you need it.

17. Pick your friends wisely. You are known by the friends you hang around with.

18. Let me know where you are, so I won't worry. If you change your plans, let me know.

19. Be careful when you drive. A car is a lethal weapon when not used safely.

20. Do your chores responsibly, on time, and without being asked.

21. Don't have anything to do with hitchhiking. Don't take or give rides to strangers.

22. Take time to know your God. Attend services at your church or temple on a regular basis.

23. Know when to stop pushing when your parents say "No." Ask for what you want, but don't become a nuisance.

24. Limit your time with television.

25. Study hard. Doing well in school and going to college are the best ways to get ahead.

26. Borrow and lend responsibly. Don't borrow without asking and return things promptly.

27. Be confident in who you are. Take pride in what you accomplish and don't put yourself down for mistakes.

28. When you are old enough to vote, vote proudly. Be a responsible citizen.

29. Have a positive attitude about life. Don't be a complainer or moody.

30. Take care of your pet or don't have one.

31. Use the phone responsibly and keep your calls a reasonable length.

32. Learn appropriate table manners and social graces.

33. Don't cheat. Play by the rules or don't play at all.

34. If you want to be successful, look the part. Good grooming and appropriate dress are important.

35. Don't take things that don't belong to you. Stealing is not acceptable. Earn the money to buy the things you want.

36. When you need your parents' help, plan for it early. Parents are not last minute servants.

37. Be polite. Being courteous means being concerned about the feelings and sensitivities of others.

38. Be on time for stated curfews and call early when there is any problem with meeting your commitments.

39. Don't put down other people. If you must gossip, keep it positive gossip.

40. Don't handle your frustrations or anger with cursing, swearing, or taking God's name in vain.

41. Listen to or read instructions before you try to do anything.

42. Keep your room clean and orderly.

43. Take care of your possessions. When you lose your own things, don't expect another to be bought for you.

44. Don't litter or abuse Mother Nature. Do your part for the environment.

OPTIONAL LECTURES (FILL OUT ONLY IF YOU ARE A TEEN WITH A BROTHER OR SISTER):

45. I'd like you two to get along. Stop fighting and work things out by talking.

46. Set a good example for your brother and sister. When you are older, you're expected to be a model.

THE LECTURE TEST ANSWER SHEET

If **TEEN**: What is your age?____What is your sex?____
List number of siblings: Brothers___; Sisters___.

If **PARENT**: What is your sex?___
Check your age range: 30-40___; 41-50___;51-60___;61-70___.

Check the number of **every lecture** message you have heard (or given) in your home in one form or another (The *content* of the message is what is important, not the *wording*)

1.__	7.__	13.__	19.__	25.__	31.__	37.__	43.__
2.__	8.__	14.__	20.__	26.__	32.__	38.__	44.__
3.__	9.__	15.__	21.__	27.__	33.__	39.__	45.__
4.__	10.__	16.__	22.__	28.__	34.__	40.__	46.__
5.__	11.__	17.__	23.__	29.__	35.__	41.__	
6.__	12.__	18.__	24.__	30.__	36.__	42.__	

ADDITIONAL QUESTIONS

List the five lectures you hear (or give) most frequently in your home: ____,____,____,____,____.

List the five lectures you hear (or give) that you feel are the most important for a teen to learn: ____,____,____,____,____.

Use the space on the back to list favorite lectures you have heard (or have used) that are funny, a catch phrase, or a unique lecture not listed in this test.

Mail to Family Lecture Research, Paulson and Associates Inc., PO Box 365, Agoura Hills, CA 91301. If you would like a short summary of the results when completed, please include your name and address.

THE LECTURE TEST ANSWER SHEET

If **TEEN**: What is your age?____What is your sex?____
List number of siblings: Brothers___; Sisters___.

If **PARENT**: What is your sex?___
Check your age range: 30-40___; 41-50___;51-60___;61-70___.

Check the number of **every lecture** message you have heard (or given) in your home in one form or another (The *content* of the message is what is important, not the *wording*)

```
1.__   7.__  13.__  19.__  25.__  31.__  37.__  43.__
2.__   8.__  14.__  20.__  26.__  32.__  38.__  44.__
3.__   9.__  15.__  21.__  27.__  33.__  39.__  45.__
4.__  10.__  16.__  22.__  28.__  34.__  40.__  46.__
5.__  11.__  17.__  23.__  29.__  35.__  41.__
6.__  12.__  18.__  24.__  30.__  36.__  42.__
```

ADDITIONAL QUESTIONS

List the five lectures you hear (or give) most frequently in your home: ____,____,____,____,____.

List the five lectures you hear (or give) that you feel are the most important for a teen to learn: ____,____,____,____,____.

Use the space on the back to list favorite lectures you have heard (or have used) that are funny, a catch phrase, or a unique lecture not listed in this test.

Mail to Family Lecture Research, Paulson and Associates Inc., PO Box 365, Agoura Hills, CA 91301. If you would like a short summary of the results when completed, please include your name and address.

So You Want to Read More?

Barbeau, Clayton. *How to Raise Parents: Questions & Answers for Teens & Parents*, Harper & Row, San Francisco, 1987.

Combs, H. Samm. *Teenage Survival Guide*, Discovery Books, Lagunitas, CA, 1989.

Davis, Ken. *How to Live with Your Parents...Without Losing Your Mind!* Zondervan, Grand Rapids, MI, 1988.

Dobson, James. *Preparing for Adolescence*, Gospel Light, Ventura, CA, 1990.

The EarthWorks Group, *50 Simple Things You Can Do to Save the Earth*, EarthWorks Press, Berkeley, CA, 1989.

Fulghum, Robert. *All I Really Need to Know I learned in Kindergarten*, Ivy Books, 1989.

Huggett, Joyce. *Dating, Sex, & Friendship*, InterVarsity Press, Downers Grove, IL, 1985.

Jensen, Eric. *Student Success Secrets*, Baron's Educational Series, Hauppauge, NY, 1982.

Peale, Norman Vincent. *Have a Great Day!* Inspirational Book Service, 66 E. Main St., Pawling, NY, 12564.

Riehm, Sarah L. *The Teenage Entrepreneur's Guide*, Surrey Books, Chicago, 1987.

Roger, John and McWilliams, Peter. *LIFE 101: Everything We Wished We Had Learned About Life in School--But Didn't*, Prelude Press, 1990.

About the Authors:

"The author who speaks about his own books is almost as bad as a mother who talks about her own children." Benjamin Disraeli

Dr. Terry L. Paulson has been described as the Will Rogers of management consulting. He prepares companies and their employees to meet the challenge of change. But few know his long background with youth, first as a teen youth worker with Young Life and many Southern California churches and then as a licensed clinical psychologist. He knows the real world teens have to face as adults, on and off the job, and he also speaks their language today. Now, with his son's help, he provides insights to prepare the next generation for the challenges every one of them will have to face. He is one of America's top-rated professional speakers presenting to young and old alike on topics ranging from self-motivation to managing conflict and change. In addition to being a father and psychologist, he is author of the popular books, *They Shoot Managers Don't They* and *Making Humor Work*. His humor and down-to-earth style that have served him well as a youth leader and professional speaker comes across on every page in this book with his son.

Sean D. Paulson has written some term papers, some good and some not so hot, but, more importantly, he has lived through most of the Paulson family lectures without any noticeable damage. He's a proud member of the Agoura High School graduating class of 1990. He's a former assistant director with the YMCA and is currently president of the So. Cal. Synod of the Youth Ministries Committee for the Evangelical Lutheran Church of America. In addition to attending his first year of college he is speaking with his dad to try to find ways to get even with him for all the things his dad has said about him from the speaking platform. He's been a teen for almost ten years, and he's not afraid to speak his piece.

Now, What Can We Do for You?

(Re)Ordering Books

Retail booksellers should order from their wholesaler or from our distributors,

Churches, non-profit organizations, public service agencies, and schools/teachers may purchase 10 or more copies at a 20% discount. Orders will be shipped postpaid. Service clubs, youth organizations and companies who may wish to distribute quantities of the books as a premium or for fund-raising purposes should contact Paulson & Associates Inc. regarding quantity discounts.

Readers, whether ordering for yourself or others, may order direct in the event the book is not available at local book stores. In such case, Paulson & Associates Inc. will forego the usual cost for "postage and handling."

Payments: Please include cheque or money order (made out to **Paulson & Associates Inc.**) with all orders.

Sales Tax: If books are to be shipped to a California address, please add 6.75% sales tax. *All sales final.* Quoted prices/discounts subject to change without notice.

ORDER OTHER BOOKS FROM THE AUTHORS:

Secrets of Life Every Teen Needs to Know
Please mail____Books at $6.95 each

Favorite Family Lectures
This is the hardcover parent/teen resource guide to all 46 of America's favorite family lectures. Family discussion questions and a lecture to parents is included. *(Available January 1991)*
Please mail____Books at $18.95 each

They Shoot Managers Don't They: Making Conflict Work in a Changing World
Dr. Paulson, with his characteristic humor and down-to-earth style, helps you manage conflict and change, increase self-esteem, handle difficult people, manage your boss, and make changes that last.
Please mail____Books at $10.95 each

Making Humor Work
Dr. Paulson's easy to read book shows how humor on the job helps develop confidence, manage stress, disarm anger, defuse resistance to change, unlock the receptivity of others and enhance communication.
Please mail____Books at $7.95 each

Name:_____

Street/P.O. Box:_____

Town:_____State:_____Zip:_____

I enclose check/money order in the amount of $_____
CA residents add 6.75% sales tax. Make payable to **Paulson & Associates Inc. Special Instructions:** (Note on the back the recipient's name and address if different from that given above.)

MAIL YOUR ORDER TO:
Paulson & Associates Inc.   **For VISA/MC Orders**
P.O. Box 365-T   **Call**
Agoura Hills, CA 91301   **(800)521-6172**